Golf

France's Most Beautiful Courses

Jean-François Bessey
Jean-François Lefèvre
Daniel Philippe

The La Bretesche Castle

Golf

*F*rance's Most Beautiful Courses

TEXT : JEAN-FRANÇOIS BESSEY
PHOTOGRAPHS : JEAN-FRANÇOIS LEFÈVRE
AND DANIEL PHILIPPE

EDITIONS TERRE D'IMAGES, CO-VISION

Front Cover:
Esterel.

Back Cover:
Etretat.

Production, lay-out and
photomechanical reproduction:
Marc Barbay, Image de Marc
Printed at Grafo, Bilbao
Registration of Copyright:
D1999/8742/2
ISBN: 90-805191-2-X

Acknowledgements
Jean-François Lefèvre particularly
wishes to extend his thanks to the
Regional Tourist Boards, the
Departmental Tourist Boards, the
Maison de France, Madame Viviane
Malgorn and the hotels recommend-
ed by the golf courses, where he
received a warm welcome. Jules
and Manon Lefèvre who patiently
awaited the return of their father
from his many journalistic forays,
must not be forgotten. Jean-François
Bessey wishes to thank Catherine
Farinati, who inspired him with the
energy to see the project through, his
parents, friends and the Thugs. We
would also like to thank Golf
Européen as well as the golf club
stewards, secretaries and all the golf
club staff who gave of their valuable
time to help us complete our project.

CONTENTS

France, Land of Golf Courses

Preface

The influence of American golfing architecture, near Deauville.△

The first hole of the Les Bordes course, a work of art in the heart of Sologne.
◁

In a year's time, a fresh page in the history of French golf will be turned as it enters the new millenium. It was in 1856 that a settlement of leisured English officers built the first golf course at Pau, the first in France and a landmark in continental golf ; since then, more than five hundred others have sprung up. Maybe with the passage of another hundred years, France may be able to boast ten times that number. But who can tell ? For the number of courses will very much depend on another bout of golf mania such as that seen in the glorious decade of the 80's, and even the most optimistic forecasts only hold for the briefest moment, a mere drop in the ocean of time. These days, there are more than three hundred thousand golfers in France. This figure appears small, but it is considerable for a country of which one never tires of repeating that it lacks the soul for this game born in the Scottish mists or on the old Dutch plains, (depending on which side of this never-ending historical squabble you place yourself).

It would be an impossible task to describe each and every one of continental France's over five hundred golf courses in this book ; an edition of several volumes would be required. The decision was therefore taken to concentrate on an edition on glossy paper spanning one hundred and fifty years of this noble sport's history, a sort of Tour de France of the country's best and most spectacular courses as they fired our imagination. With their elegant greens, merciless bunkers, challenging reed-fringed water hazards, magnificent vistas and clubhouse comforts, French golf courses are no longer the poor relations of their Anglo-Saxon cousins. The beauty and variety of these courses have seduced the British and the Scandinavians, furnishing the proof, shown in the following pages, that France is indeed a land of golf courses.

The Basque Coast

The Biarritz Nursery

The Basque Coast

Wedged between the Atlantic Ocean and the Pyrenees, the French Basque coast is the cradle of French golf. It was here that all the French champions over the last century from Arnaud Massy to Marie-Laure de Lorenzi learned to take their first swing. This is the country of the chistera, discoid crosses and elvers, where a proud people and well-watered fairways are waiting to be discovered.

It is impossible to miss the entrance to the Chantaco golf course where so many French professionals began their golfing career.

△

On the sea front, fences have been erected to prevent the sand from overwhelming Chiberta's fairways.

◁

Following pages:
A landmark for sailors, the light-house from which Biarritz golf course takes its name, is also a reference point for the golfers of Biarritz and Chiberta.

◁◁

It was in the nineteenth century, on a strip of undulating land on the French Basque coast between the Pyrenees and the Atlantic, generously watered by rains coming in off the ocean, that French golf was born. "Not so," retort pernickety historians. "The first clumsy golf swings were taken in 1856, when the first golf course on continental Europe opened in Pau." The first golfers in mainland France were, of course, inhabitants of the Béarn - or rather subjects of Her Gracious Majesty, The Queen of the British Empire, but it was on the banks of the river Nive, thirty or forty years later, that golf reached its apogee.

The well-to-do families and officers garrisoned in the Béarn capital had considered golf as merely an agreeable pastime; it took the Basques to make it a fully-fledged sport. To understand and master it, they turned to their native traditions. Confronting bulls in the arena had given them a sense of strategy, the pelota an ample swing and Basque trials of strength a powerful drive.

One century has been enough for the Basques to make it to the top of the roll call of French golf. From Arnaud Massy to Marie-Laure de Lorenzi, the sons of Biarritz and Saint-Jean-de-Luz have brought back the most coveted titles to their clubs. Yellowing photographs on the walls of the clubhouses testify to these feats of golfing skill. Silver trophies in their cabinets have lost none of their shine.

For the French Basque country takes pride in its champions. It is proud of the willpower and courage of its sons who have brought to the four corners of the earth a human warmth which is the legacy of back-breaking work in the fields and long voyages at sea. It is proud, too, of the tough men who carried golf

bags for rich families on holiday in Biarritz, and who spent their evenings hitting cheap rubber balls by candlelight.

In days gone by, caddies would sit in the cafés in the evenings and, with glasses of Iroulégy in their calloused hands, strike up songs echoed by their cheerful companions.

In the mornings they would follow the road to the Biarritz-le-Phare golf club along the cliffs of La Chambre d'Amour. At the caddy-master's hut, they would wait for the golfers for whom they would work that day. As a mark of homage to these pioneers, the century-old golf club erected, on the gravel pathway leading to the clubhouse, a statue to former caddy Arnaud Massy, the only French winner of the golf tournament par excellence, The British Open, on the fearsome links at Hoylake in England in 1907. The modest bronze statue, however, was coveted by the champion's most fervent admirers and

Founded in 1888, the Biarritz-le-Phare golf course is now within striking distance of the town. The locals live at the very foot of the fairways.

Designed by Pierre Thévenin, Ilbarritz's nine holes and its training centre look out over the Atlantic ocean. △

At Biarritz-le-Phare, the greens are small and the bunkers judiciously placed. ◁

disappeared from its pedestal one night. The golf club committee, outraged by this sacrilege, immediately commissioned an identical copy of the original.

Biarritz-le-Phare, established in 1888, epitomises the golf clubs of the last century. Designed by the English architect, Tom Dunn, and slightly modified by H.S. Colt, the course, these days within a stone's throw of the town, is only five thousand three hundred and seventy six metres long and has tiny putting

Biarritz-le-Phare is battered by Atlantic winds. This makes the relatively short course seem rather long.

greens. It is a striking contrast to the American architecture which has been invading mainland France since the 1970's. At Biarritz-le-Phare the boldest players even try to reach some par four greens with their driver in one shot. At their own risk ! For there are many cunningly placed bunkers waiting to swallow up balls carried off course by the whims of the Atlantic winds.

Whether as a result of respect or a stroke of genius, this golf club is today twinned with Augusta in Georgia, USA, the world's most famous golfing town after St. Andrews. Every April, it hosts one of the four major tournaments, the Masters on the Augusta National course. In the trophy cabinet in the restaurant of the Biarritz-le-Phare clubhouse hangs the yellow flag of the Augusta National which was carefully brought back by Denis Lalanne, a native of Biarritz and former star reporter on the newspaper L'Equipe, to testify to this prestigious connection.

Whilst the other regions of France were waking up to golf at a leisurely pace, the French Basque coast was alive with various projects. Before the nineteenth century was out, a second golf course had been designed by the Baron de l'Espée, just outside Biarritz in the borough of Bidart. Work started in 1914, but was destroyed by fire in the First World War. Saint-Jean-le-Luz saw the building of the nine-hole Sainte-Barbe course in 1893, only for it to succumb, a few years later, to the tempting offers of prestige property developers, who were even then on the scene. Out of the remains of the Sainte-Barbe course was born the La Nivelle course in the borough of Ciboure, a fishing port bordering on Saint-Jean-de-Luz, part of a never-ending cycle of resurrections. La Nivelle's fairways unfurl at the foot of the Rhune massif, undulating upwards to the summit from where, between swings, visitors can delight in the magnificent views over the ocean and the Pyrenees.

After a period of exile in Paris at La Boulie golf club, Arnaud Massy, originally from Biarritz, returned to his native soil and chose the first floor of La Nivelle's

The golf pro-shop of La Nivelle golf course : Arnaud Massy lived on its first floor for many years. △△

As a tribute to the great champion, winner of the British Open in 1907, the town of Ciboure named the road running along La Nivelle golf course after him. △

La Nivelle is cut by valleys. Choosing a club for the greens below is a delicate matter.
◁

golf pro-shop as his base. This return to his roots enabled him to pass on his knowledge of the game and his skill with the "cane" (as clubs used to be known) to younger players. It was thanks to this exceptional player and teacher that La Nivelle became the cradle of Basque golf. Arnaud Massy was authoritarian, inflexible, a hard taskmaster. Nevertheless, once school was over, the children from the houses near the Basque chalet Lohobia, which had become the clubhouse, hurried to his master classes and followed them intently. These youngsters, who themselves became teachers, for example, Garaialde, Palli, Alsugüren, Saubaber, then spread his gospel across the whole of France. The Basques were everywhere from Fontainebleau to Cannes, from Lyon to Brest.

Arnaud Massy then re-embarked on his pilgrimage and established himself at the Etretat golf club in the Seine Maritime, which he never left. When he died at the age of eighty-one, the municipality of Ciboure named the road bordering La Nivelle golf club in his honour. The former caddy had become a figure equal in stature to the other great personnage of Ciboure, the composer Maurice Ravel. Only in the Basque country could such an honour be done to golf.

The homage paid to the origins of golf at the Chiberta course in Anglet comes with the territory, a homage to its first courses, called links, which were built along the sea-shore in the sands of the dunes. Tom Simpson, one of the masters of English architecture, was able subtly to marry holes situated in pine-woods with a six-hole sequence along the sea front. This combination means that golf-lovers have to stretch their repertoire to shots unheard of on other Basque courses. Tom Simpson was however only acting on the orders of his employer, the Duke of Windsor, "Sir, I wish you to create the most beautiful golf course in the world on this land." It was a bold challenge. Chiberta did not become one of the most beautiful golf courses in the world, but the fact that nowadays it is one of the most visited courses in France speaks volumes.

In Chiberta the route from the teeing ground to the hole is not always a straight line. One has to know how to take account of the elements to keep the ball in play. It is important to know how to "work" the ball, to make it turn to the left or to the right, to make it leave the tee low against the wind and to make the most of advice given by the regulars. This is why, at the fourteenth hole, a long par five by the beach, the locals will urge you to drive aiming straight

The green of the second hole at Ilbarritz, the most spectacular nine holes in France. The Rhune and the Jaizikibel can be seen in the distance.

Chiberta, with its fairways built in the dunes, is one of the few links on the Atlantic coast.

towards the Biarritz lighthouse, which means straight out to sea, so that the prevailing wind will carry the ball in a graceful curve back onto the fairway.

While the golfers have to battle with the gusty winds off the ocean, the course itself endeavours to put up resistance to the sands which are stealthily winning ground from the golf course. After the vines from which vin de sable was made were cut down, trees protected the course from the shoreline. However, these were felled by German soldiers to build the Atlantic Wall during the Second World War.

To stem the encroaching sands, Gironde barriers have been erected on the borders of the rough. Many visitors would like to see these wooden fences, which block the view of the ocean rollers, removed, but without these protective measures the sands would swallow up the fairways, transforming the extraordinary par five fourteenth hole into a giant four hundred and thirty seven metre bunker.

Founded in 1926, the Chiberta golf course's golden age was in the 1930's. Its carpark was crammed with long limousines whose chauffeurs gathered in a bar, specially built for them, to kill the long hours until their masters would come back, their faces ruddy with sea-spray. Then, a long period of decline set in and the fairways became overgrown with clover. Chiberta was in its death-throes and lay forgotten until the 1970's, until, under the stewardship of Jean-Baptiste Ellisalde, the Anglet club determinedly embarked upon the long process of gradually winning back, year by year, both the hearts of the golfers and the club's former glory. Today, in spite of a tiny clubhouse which some people have no hesitation in finding ill-suited to such a marvellous course and a practice course at the water's edge inappropriate for training, Chiberta once more boasts a rude health. For in addition to having many members of its own, enough to make other French golf club managers pale with envy, it also welcomes visitors daily. As an older member notes, times have changed, "Twenty years ago, you didn't have to wait to tee off from the first hole."

Basque golf is a men's story. At Chantaco it could even be said to be one family's story. Three generations of it have left their mark on the jewel of Saint-Jean-de Luz. Three syllables, La-co-ste, were to make an international name for themselves and the most famous member of the family, René, was active in three areas. He was a great tennis player in the 1930's, creator of the shirt bearing the famous green crocodile and owner of the Chantaco golf club. The family is revered and respected by the forty-four professionals trained at Chantaco. When they mention the tennis hero, they refer to him with bated

Behind the green of Chiberta's first hole, the pink Moorish-style palace conjures up dreams of far away places.
▽

The Chantaco club-house. Inside it is an art deco master-piece.
◁

For seventy years, Chantaco has belonged to the same family, the Lacostes, creators of sportswear marked with the green crocodile.

breath as "Monsieur Lacoste". To respect for the father can also be added that earned by his daughter Catherine, who was nicknamed "Catherine the Great" by an American journalist the day after winning the women's US Golf Open in 1967, whilst still only an amateur.

This family legend will ensure that Chantaco remains unique in French golf. Chantaco has never changed hands since it first opened in 1928 with an exhibition match between the French team of Arnaud Massy and Jean Gassiat and the English brothers Percy and Audrey Boomer. Its founder, René Thion de la Chaume, simply passed the family legacy on to his daughter Simone, wife of René Lacoste. " Catherine the Great ", today club President, need not worry; fourteen grandchildren mean that the course will be taken over by someone in the family so that Chantaco and its fourteen thousand trees will continue to perpetuate the family tradition and the spirit of the game.

In Arcangues, one family's spirit has been passed down over a millenium. The Arcangues family, who gave their name to this delightful little village in the Basque hinterland, have been inhabitants of the area since 1150. The family castle overshadows the fifteenth hole of this new golf course opened in 1991. Guy d'Arcangues, a former member of the French amateur team, headed the family project of creating a golf course which would keep the family estates intact and head off the property developers. For this picturesque village, where many Parisians come to get married, was attracting the interest of investors.

As in Bassussary, another course built in the 1990's, an American was chosen to design the course. From the clubhouse terrace which looks towards the Pyrenees, the sloping fairways, wide bunkers and water hazards are visible, testifying to a complex design full of variety.

On the church square, between the fronton and the inns whose half-timbers are dyed with bulls' blood, the discoid steles of finely-worked stone in the small cemetery where the singer Luis Gonzalez, alias Luis Mariano, is buried, bear witness to the mystery surrounding the Basque people whose origins date back to the dawn of time.

No new course has opened in Bayonne and Biarritz in the last eight years. Could this be a sign of the decline of Basque golf ? Decidedly not. Even though the golf nursery of yesteryear, the caddies, has disappeared, the new

The American Ronald Fream designed the Arcangues course on the ancestral lands of the Arcangues family.

Chantaco's first hole, starting point for a golfing walk of five thousand seven hundred and twenty two metres. In their childhood, dozens of budding professionals followed the same route.
◁◁

Bassussary is the most recent Basque golf course. Its wide fairways are a paradise for strong hitters. The par threes, however, demand a much more subtle approach.
◁/▽

generation of golfers works on its swing in the training centres of Ilbarritz or on the rustic fairways of the little golf course at Epherra. These students are no longer sons of peasants or fishermen. Although not fired with their ancestors' desire to conquer, they have gained their experience, an invaluable fund of knowledge passed down during family evenings in long tales of tournaments, extraordinary shots and journeys to the four corners of Europe. One hundred epic years without which French golf would not exist.

The singer Luis Mariano is buried in the cemetery at Arcangues, which overlooks the golf course.
△

La Nivelle's fairways overlooking the pretty port of Saint-Jean-de-Luz.
◁◁

Chiberta is not only a links. There are some holes amidst the trees.
▽

*L*anguedoc-Roussillon

Spontaneous Generation

Languedoc Roussillon

In the 1980's the region of Languedoc-Roussillon, stretching from Nîmes to the Pyrenees, merely sold itself on sunshine. But that was before its decision to turn itself into a golfer's paradise. Now you can wander Mediterranean fairways from the Petite Camargue to the Cathar castles.

Mount Canigou and its snow-covered peaks has given its name to the eighteen-hole course of Saint-Cyprien. △

At one thousand one hundred metres above sea-level, Falgos is the last golf course of the Eastern Pyrenees before Spain. ◁

Preceding pages: The pretty port of Collioure provided inspiration for the Fauvist painters.

The Falgos golf course in the heart of the Pyrenees is the last stop before Spain. The air is pure and the light clear. It stands at an altitude of one thousand one hundred metres in a wooded estate of six hundred and fifty hectares. The road winds steeply upwards to the Domaine de Falgos terminus, beyond which the only mountain thoroughfares are the fairways of this impeccably maintained eighteen-hole course and paths for electric buggies. The view from the hotel terrace is magnificent, taking in, to the left, the bay of Rosace unfolding into the Mediterranean, and the Spanish villages of Cadaquès and Figueras, birthplace of the Surrealist painter Salvador Dali, and, to the right, the snow-capped peaks of the Canigou. Although the earliest human remains, a three hundred and twenty thousand year old skull, were unearthed in the Arago grotto in Tautavel (the Eastern Pyrenees), the golfing age in the Languedoc-Roussillon is as yet in its early infancy. Falgos is the latest in a line of courses that sprang up as if by spontaneous generation at the end of the 1980's.

Whilst the French Riviera and the Basque coast had long looked to their golf links to entice new French and foreign customers who had money to spend, Languedoc-Roussillon lived only off its sandy beaches and its three hundred days of sunshine per year. With its reputation as a cheap summer holiday destination, the region's camping and caravan sites proliferated. This is an image which the people of Languedoc are keen to dispel. Over in La Grande-Motte, they worry that old beliefs die hard. "After all, there's more to Languedoc-Roussillon than wind, mosquitoes and caravans !" they thunder. A visit to the pretty town of Aigues-Mortes in Hérault, a fortified port established by Louis IX (Saint Louis)or to Collioure, home of the Fauvist painters, will persuade you of the justice of this claim. Not to mention the

treasures of the Gard region with its famous Roman bridge built two thousand years ago on the orders of Agrippa, son-in-law to the Emperor Augustus, and Nîmes where the oldest Roman arenas in France can be found. A town of many epithets - Roman, Medieval, ancien régime, modern – Nîmes is a living history book in itself.

The first golf course to open in Languedoc-Roussillon, Nîmes-Campagne, has drawn on the riches of history to create a legend for itself. For when the time comes for a pastis, the ritual apéritif is spun round with fabulous tales. It is whispered that the treasure of the Knights Templar may be buried under a lush fairway, in the undergrowth or beneath the foundations of the clubhouse, a miniature White House in the purest Washington style.

These great riches accumulated by the Order of the Knights Templar whet the treasure hunters' appetite. Nobody knows if it really exists, but everyone likes to dream that it does, for Nîmes- Campagne is built on land once used as a resting place for Knights returning from the Crusades with their booty. It was amidst these ancient trees that the magician-like Tito Lassalle imparted the art of golf to some of French golf's finest pros. A difficult task given the lack of other golf courses elsewhere in the area. For almost twenty years Nîmes-Campagne was the sole symbol of golf in Languedoc-Roussillon until the region, which had been neglected by high-class tourism, caught the eye of the promoters. In architects' offices, plans of holiday villages were sketched out on drawing boards. Builders of the brave new world of the 1960's dreamt up dazzling new

At La Grande Motte the course is flat, but the many water hazards make it dificult to negotiate.

cities. La Grande-Motte rose up from the earth of the Petite Camargue, its famous appartment-pyramids on the waterfront paying their creator's tribute to the Mexican temples of Teotihuacan. Green areas, bicycle lanes, ample parking facilities, La Grande-Motte, brainchild of the Prime Minister's cousin, Jean Balladur, can claim to be a futurist city. This unrestrained urbanism makes plenty of allowance for sports complexes and in 1987 the American architect Robert Trent Jones came to Montpellier to put the

A typical par three in the American style designed by Robert Trent Jones on the Flamands Roses course at La Grande Motte.

Property surrounds Massane's first holes. The discreet presence of the houses does not, however, spoil the beauty of the course.

Preceding pages: La Grande Motte is dotted with marshes which provide sanctuary for the great wader birds during migrations.

finishing touches to La Grande Motte course. It comprises forty-one holes, divided into three courses, one with six practice holes, one "executive" course with eighteen holes and no bunker and one championship course, Flamands Roses. The golf novices of Montpellier and La Grande Motte made swift progress on these instructive courses. Holding the AGF Open there with entry cards to the European circuit further contributed to raising the profile of this complex both in France and abroad. These days, Languedoc-Roussillon is thriving on the custom of foreign golfers. Germans, British, Swedes and Swiss have found an alternative to Andalucia, crowded and swelteringly hot in summer. Here, green-fees are half the price, the sun shines and the sea is only a few kilometres away.

Meanwhile, the firm of Jeanjean, a family owned public works company, is launching Montpellier-Massane. As in La Grande-Motte, a discreet building programme is allowing golf to live and to flourish. "We are no

Massane is home to the David Leadbetter Golf Academy. Its students practise daily on the difficult multi-level greens.

philanthropists," proclaim the two brothers. "We like golf, but without the two hundred and fifty houses which are only visible from the first holes, Montpellier-Massane would not exist." The Jeanjeans brought back Ronald Fream with them from Tunisia, where they had gone to build football pitches. The American architect has one maxim : "A beautiful golf course should look its best at sunset when the shadows lengthen. If it doesn't, the course is badly designed." To play at hide-and-seek with the sun, Ronald Fream has gently moulded the old vineyards and orchards into mounds and

raised greens which reveal the light's magic when the sun's rays slip below the horizon. Not only is the American concerned with the aesthetics of twilight in his first French creation, he also puts the player under pressure immediately at hole number five, a par five with its island green offering two options (caution or attack) for the second shot. In competition, this is the most feared hole and the five to six hundred red carp in the water hazard are often disturbed by balls smashing like meteorites into its depths.

In La Grande Motte the seventh hole sorts the sheep from the goats : a par five which also finishes on an island green. "You either come through the hole unscathed or come off the green with double figures on your scorecard. And with eleven still to play, the afternoon can become a nightmare," say the connoisseurs at the clubhouse bar, savouring a plate of tellines, types of shellfish marinaded in white wine and garlic, with their apéritif.

From Saint-Cyprien to the Cap d'Agde, La Grande Motte to Montpellier-Massane, foreign golfers play to their heart's content. The coastal golf links with their friendly atmospheres, reasonable green fees and their pleasant, although not state of the art, courses exploit their cosmopolitan appeal to the utmost. However, in Carcassonne, a fortified town which seems to be taken straight out of Orson Welles' Falstaff, the golf course is seldom visited. And yet the city of Carcassonne, a jewel of medieval architecture surrounded by three kilometres of ramparts and fifty-two crenellated towers, is mentioned in all the guide books. The surrounding area is home to the Cathar castles, impregnable fortresses built atop dizzying heights, which delight children and parents alike and which recall an episode of French history stained with the blood of sacrificial victims.

The Carcassonne golf course, built on the Auriac estate, mirrors these military edifices surrounded by moats and stone walls. The Basque, Jean-Pierre Basurco, club pro turned golf architect for the occasion, has placed the tee of the number one hole in front of a grassy mound which has to be cleared with a hefty wood shot to reach a plateau covered by winding fairways. On the return, the ninth hole is a small par three protected by the Saint-Jean brook to which one tees off from a high vantage point. It is the very mirror-image of Carcassonne and its impregnable ramparts. Although the Pyrenees range, with its black mountains, can be made out on the horizon on a clear day, the city of Carcassonne, but a stone's throw away,

Thousands of golfers in search of a training position have crossed the threshold of the Saint-Cyprien clubhouse.
▽

Be careful of venturing off the fairways of Saint-Cyprien. On Canigou's sixteenth hole is a sign warning of quicksand.
◁

The club professional, the Basque Jean Pierre Basurco, designs this very pretty Carcassonne course.

is carefully concealed by the undulating terrain. Nonetheless, one of the club brochures shows a picture of a flagstick fluttering like a banner against a background of watchtowers and machicolations. A simple photographic montage which fools nobody but the most gullible and which Jo Riu, happily retired from the footwear industry and now President and Treasurer of the only club in Aude, finds highly amusing. Unable fully to abandon the pleasures of commerce, Jo Riu purchased some vine plots and now produces the Domaine des Bouziers, a Cabernet-Sauvignon with the striped JR label, which can be found meticulously lined up on the clubhouse tables.

On feast days in Falgos, guests quaff pourron de Muscat and eat cargolade (large grilled snails) on tables set up in the open air around the

ninth green. The light from film projectors cuts a luminous tunnel through the thick darkness and the practice green in front of the hotel takes on magical hues. On these summer evenings, laughter, the whistle of golf balls and the crackling of the wood fire are the only sounds to break the silence of the Pyrenees. Here, one can make merry without the fear of causing disturbance, for in Falgos, one is at the ends of the earth.

At the Carcassonne course, the Black Mountain can be seen on the horizon when the sky is clear.

The French Riviera

A Scent of Mimosa

The French Riviera from Menton to Toulon is the region of France most prized by golfers in search of sunshine, warm seas and golfing greens perfumed with the scent of mimosa flowers. Enthusiasm for the sport was sown by a noble of the Russian court. St. Petersburg is no St. Andrews, but in true visionary fashion, the Grand Duke spread his passion for golf from Cannes to Sperone in Corsica.

The tribute in stone to the founder of Cannes-Mandelieu, Grand Duke Michael of Russia.
△

Before becoming the Cannes-Mandelieu clubhouse, this half-timbered building was a hunting lodge.
◁

Preceding pages: Vence, in the Nice hinterland, is a charming village nestling in the flower-covered hills of Provence
◁◁

For millions of refugees forced to leave the land of their birth, exile is a wound that scars the soul. One fine day in 1879, Grand Duke Michael and his wife, Countess Sophie de Turby, granddaughter of the great poet Pushkin, received orders to leave Russian territory. An order from Czar Alexander III brooked no discussion. In spite of the Napoleonic Wars of the early nineteenth century, France had lost none of her appeal. For well-educated Russians, the blow of exile was softened somewhat by residence in France and yearnings for home were perhaps less urgent.

Their hearts heavy with the knowledge that they were leaving Mother Russia never to return, Grand Duke Michael and his family chose to settle in the Mediterranean seaside town of Cannes, a favourite summer holiday destination of the European aristocracy.

Once settled in the Villa des Dunes, Grand Duke Michael set about re-creating the splendours of the St. Petersburg court. Festivity upon festivity was held, each one more magnificent than the last. Life was a social whirl, decadent, probably identical to the scenes described so wonderfully by the Norman writer Jean Lorrain in his novel, Les Noronsoff.

One day, worn out with this orgy of pleasure, Grand Duke Michael and his wife decided to grant themselves a respite – a holiday in England and Scotland that was to become a journey of initiation into the land of golf. It was either chance or destiny that brought the Grand Duke to St. Andrew's, the capital of Scottish golf. Whilst out on a partridge shoot, he caught sight through the trees of the venerable links of the Old Course, whose fairways blend seamlessly with the shoreline of the Eden estuary. The Grand Duke lowered his gun and watched intrigued as golfers hit balls with their hickory-handled clubs towards flagsticks clattering in the Scottish sea wind. This encounter was to leave a life-long mark.

Back in France at the Villa des Dunes, he regaled guests at his famous dinners with his growing passion for this sport as yet unknown on the Riviera. With some friends who had come to share his enthusiasm, he established the Cannes Golf Club, buying some hectares of land by the Mediterranean to build the first links on the Riviera, a nine-hole green in the shade of parasol pines.

Given that the all the first golf clubs on the French mainland were established by the English, the founding of the Cannes-Mandelieu golf club by a noble of the Russian court is not without its piquancy. The Grand Duke Michael had even beaten Lord Ashcomb to it, the founder of the Valescure club at St. Raphaël in 1895, and so the Cannes Golf Club became, after Pau-Billière and Biarritz-le-Phare, the third oldest golf club in France.

The subjects of Her Gracious Majesty, however, did not hold it against him and a group of British army colonels took over the sporting organisation of the club, imbuing the club with a very British feel. Champagne glasses were not smashed against the wall as they were in St. Petersburg. The tendancy was more towards afternoon tea, china tea-cups held with one's little finger raised. And to provide a few drops of luke-warm milk for this precious beverage, a cow was allowed to graze on the fairways. Cannes-Mandelieu cultivated country chic.

These carefree times for the European aristocracy were, however, to come to an abrupt end with the devastating flames of the two world wars which bloodily marked the nineteenth century. The course was long to suffer from its war-wounds, for before it was decided to re-open the course in the 1950's, twenty thousand mines had to be dug out of the lawns of its fairways.

In the post-war years, the Riviera became the ultimate place to be seen and was marked by every new extravagance. Roger Vadim's film, And God created Woman, which brought the sex-kitten Brigitte Bardot to fame, triggered an enthusiasm for the little port of St. Tropez in the Var and each spring the Cannes film Festival brings La Croisette to prominence under the flash-bulbs of publicity. Each summer in the 1950's and 60's, Parisians

hurried down to the south coast on the number seven motorway, a legendary road, synonymous with summer holidays and sung about so tenderly by Charles Trénet. France is now slowly returning to more civilised leisure pursuits.

Now enlarged to eighteen holes, the Cannes-Mandelieu golf club, which is set to become France's most visited course, is now threatened by a camping

Cannes-Mandelieu's fairways are fringed with parasol pines. Their shade brings some cool air to the oldest course on the Riviera.

ground. On the river Siagne, the little ferry boat which connects the second and third holes and the twelfth and thirteenth holes, carries its cargo of golfers under the mocking eyes of campers. The battle has raged for months, even reaching the local council. The councillors, however, have sufficient vision to recognise the importance of a golf course for the tourist development of a holiday town. Cannes-Mandelieu has felt the heat. The soon-to-be hundred year old very nearly passed away on turning sixty.

The paradox of the Riviera is that whilst it has over two hundred kilometres of Mediterranean coastline, very few of its courses have views over the sea. This is because of the geographical constraints of the Var where the ochre cliffs of the Maure and Estérel ranges plunge straight down into the Mediterranean. Economic constraints are also imposed by the coastal strip of the Alpes-Maritimes being so monopolised by real estate that property prices per square metre have rocketed.

As a consequence, golf clubs have taken to the higher ground, to sloping and rocky terrain where the architects have had to employ their imagination to the full in creating putting greens and fairways.

Monte-Carlo's golf club and the Principality's coat of arms. △◁

Monte-Carlo's fairways on Mount Agel seem to reach the sky. △

Royal Mougins's second hole invites the player to take the "Angel's Leap", but it is better to overhit than to end up short of the green. ▷

The Cannes-Mougins clubhouse. In its opulent lounge are oil presses dating from 1836.

Already at the beginning of the century, the Monte-Carlo golf club had been built at over eight hundred metres, on the top of Mount Agel - quite a task at the time. To achieve such a tour de force, hundreds of labourers went up to Mount Agel at the beginning of spring and worked without a break until autumn.

At night, they slept outside in the open air or in a tent. After several years of work, the eighteen holes were opened on November 16th 1911.

Royal Mougins employs two full-time gardeners to maintain the flower beds. △

Once the morning mists have dispersed, the Monte Carlo golf club boasts a wonderful view over the Mediterranean, even taking in the Italian coast. It is without doubt the course with a view of the "French Riviera".

Thomas Levet, the French professional, has wonderful memories of Royal Mougins. He won the Cannes Open on its winding fairways in 1998. ◁

Few other coastal golf courses enjoy such a location. Only La Frégate in the Var offers fortunate visitors the chance to take a few drives towards the Mediterranean from the second hole. On this course, with its testing relief and difficult green approaches, the sea is not the only match companion. Some holes go around the Domaine de la Frégate vineyards. This winery with the appelation Bandol is independent of the club, but its produce can be savoured on the clubhouse terrace, creating the perfect marriage of birdies and wine-tasting.

The second half of the Sainte-Maxime course or the extension of the old Beauvallon course also offers views of the Mediterranean , but these coveted views are only small windows through the barriers of hills or dense parasol pines.

Other new courses can be found further inland, several kilometres from the coast, such as Royal Mougins, the third course to be built in Cannes after the Cannes-Mandelieu and Cannes-Mougins. It opened in 1963 and has hosted eleven

Cannes Opens. Today, professionals play for this European circuit title on the Royal-Mougins' new undulating fairways designed by the American Robert Van Hagge.

Opened in 1993, Royal-Mougins could have seen the light of day almost eighty years earlier when the Englishman Lord Wilson visited his close friend, the Count de Pourtalès. In the estate's higher areas, Lord Wilson discovered the little villages of Mougins, Mandelieu - La Napoule and La Roquette and instantly fell in love with them. This English nobleman never went anywhere without his golf clubs. He imagined fairways leading to the Vallon de l'Oeuf and hit some balls into the wild grasses. Eighty years later Robert Van Hagge did not deviate from this vision on being shown the land for the course just purchased by the Norwegian promoter Otto Berg.

On the architect's drawing board, the sculpting of the lawn took shape where the light plays at cat and mouse with the lush green slopes of its fairways and greens. They represent visual traps for over-confident players. A course of high golfing stakes, Royal Moulins's second hole, a par three, demands a stroke of heroic proportions to make the ball drop sharply down onto the green. The hole is called "Angel's Leap", but beware of the landing !

The "natural" course of Saint-Endréol is also one which tests the balance of the golfer's swing. Its architect, Michel Gayon, wanted to play on the golfers' nerves. From the opening tee to the thirteenth hole, the view plunges down to a green surrounded with stones thirty metres below, a fortress of green velvet, protected by a stream. To reach it the iron stroke demands precision and a perfect alignment towards the hole.

This is what is the specialists call "a signature hole" by which they mean the hole shown on all the postcards and the symbol of golf in the hinterland of the Var. A par three, which moves the golfer between fear and admiration, and, in competition, to exasperation, as one ball after another drops into the water hazard, a magnet for any shot which is too tentative.

Fortunately the architects have not designed too many of these famous signature holes, the photographer's delight, but the average golfer's nightmare.

Whichever, the stroll at Saint-Endréol is well worth a few unsuccessful swings, for the strength of the course is that it immerses the player in

Preceding pages: Saint-Endréol is a long way from the coastal bustle. This course is steeped in calm and love of nature.

The Saint-Endréol course is framed by the Rouet hills and the Rocher de Roquebrune.
◁

In the Var hinterland, the Taulune golf course is one thousand metres above sea-level. Designed by the South African, Gary Player, it cost almost two hundred million francs !
▷▷

The Estérel massif and pine trees are the golfer's companion throughout the eighteen holes of the Estérel course. ▷

Barbaroux is Pete Dye's only French course.

La Grande Bastide was designed by Cabell Robinson and commissioned by the Club Med for its clients in the village of Opio.

The clubhouse and hotel of Taulune were opened with a great fanfare. That day, the coming and going of Ferraris and helicopters aroused the notice of the neighbouring village. ▽

natural surroundings, preserved for the moment at least, from this region's encroaching property development. It comprises a walk of over six kilometres amidst pine and broom trees to the heady chirruping of the cicadas; if at Saint-Endréol, one turns one's back to the Mediterranean for a moment, the horizon is filled with the Rocher de Roquebrune, the Rouet hills and the mountains of the Haut-Var.

The strength of the Riviera, a golfers' paradise, is not only the considerable number of courses (almost thirty), but also in the quality of its golfing architects. No other region of France has attracted as many great names—Gary Player at Taulane, Severiano Ballasteros at Pont-Royal, in the Bouches-du-Rhone, Pete Dye at Barbaroux, Cabell Robinson at La Grande Bastide … not to mention the all-time-great, Robert Trent Jones, designer of more than five hundred golf courses all over the world and the inventor of modern golf architecture. On the Riviera, his first creative work was on the forty hectares of pine wood in the Estérel massif. This was brought to final fruition in his masterpiece, the Sperone golf course on the southern tip of Corsica, a few kilometres from Bonifacio.

Preceding pages: The old Valescure hotel, which welcomed Winston Churchill in its time, overlooks the nearby Estérel course.

◁◁

Power of the Imagination

Rhône Alpes

Stretching from southern Burgundy to snow-capped Alpine summits, the Rhône-Alpes region is synonymous with wine, fine food and voluptuous fairways. On this land of plains and mountains, the golf architects have been able to give free rein to their creativity.

The foot-shaped green and the toe-shaped bunkers of the Mâcon-la-Salle course. △

The snow-covered peaks of the Alps and verdant fairways meet on the Chamonix course. ◁

In the mountains irons are preferred to the woods. ▷

Preceding pages: Above the Alps rises the four thousand eight hundred and seven metre Mont Blanc. ◁◁

Well-informed wine connoisseurs say that Mâcon wines are full-bodied, elegant and rounded. Maybe it was whilst savouring a pouilly-fuissé or a juliénas that the architect Robert Berthet sketched out his course at Mâcon-la-Salle ? Or was it his amorous adventures which inspired this course with its suggestive curves ? "A client with a bit of nerve as well as a suitable site were still necessary to bring the idea to fruition. Patrick de la Chesnais was willing to back it. And the site, La Salle in Burgundy, seemed to fit all the criteria as a region of fine food, great essential wines and undulating hills," wrote the architect in an edition of France Golf, specially dedicated to the "eternal feminine". Eighteeen holes are laid out in homage to the human form, its greens and bunkers in the form of feet and hands, the zones between the teeing ground and the fairway like long, slender legs sheathed in dark green … a golf course which truly attains its erotic dimension when seen from the air. At ground level the forms seem to shrink away from prying eyes.

At Mâcon-la-Salle, the feminine form is not only exalted by the artist's pencil; nature provides its finery. "The rough is her clothing. In some

Near Magève is the Mont d'Arbois course and its alpine fairways. △

Isola 2000's most beautiful par three with its green surrounded by lush vegetation. ◁

places it's a veil, others a light covering (the golfers call it "the short stuff") draped over the body; in some places she has a thick fur coat of broom trees and roses and in others her hair is a mass of fruit trees. Around the eleventh green she even has a string of "apple-bunkers" like a necklace, …"

In the Rhône-Alpes region, architects have also brought their imagination to courses in the mountains. Skiers and snowboarders schussing down the mountains in winter have no idea that their acrobatics are describing the generous lips of a bunker covered with thick snow. Building a course on slopes of such impressively varying heights may appear an impossible task. The first person to take up this challenge in France was the Englishman Henry Cotton, who created the Mont d'Arbois course in 1923 at an altitude of almost one thousand three hundred metres.Then, sixty years later, it was the turn of Robert Trent Jones, who built the Chamonix golf club in the magnificent setting of Mont Blanc and the Aiguilles Rouges. It was quite a task – and still is – given the very short period in which work can be carried out (June to October) and the short period in which the complex can make an income (at best, three months a year). In contrast to Méribel, the course is quite flat and

At Chamonix, Robert Trent Jones has paved the way for other Alpine golf courses. This relatively flat course winds between streams and the Arve.
◁

At the Gouverneur, the numerous ponds become fishing grounds. You need both your golf clubs and fishing rods!▷

The Gouverneur clubhouse is located in the outbuildings of Breuil castle.
△

is used for cross-country ski-ing in the winter. In spite of these limitations mountain golf courses have proliferated : there are eleven in the regions of Isère, Savoie and Haute-Savoie. Golf and new leisure activities such as mountain-biking, water-rafting or para-gliding have allowed the ski resorts, which have traditionally only been able to make their living during the winter months, to diversify their tourist revenues and to make a living during two seasons rather than one. It is not uncommon for a greenkeeper to put on his ski equipment in the winter to work as a ski instuctor. Two seasons – two jobs.

Golfers also have a new way of enjoying their hobby, for playing on a mountain is not the same as playing on the flat. The driver is not the most popular club; at the teeing ground the irons are preferred, being more precise and easier to control. The ball travels higher and for longer, an important criterion in choosing a club. The slopes also play a considerable role in game strategy and on the putting greens, the slopes always lead into the valley. In the mountains, old certainties have to be abandoned. Here the pleasure of playing is more important than the scorecard, for the concentration is distracted by the beauty of the unsullied landscape. In the mountains, one can take one's time because the fairways of these courses, which, with a touch of irony, some refer to as "goat terrain" are too steep to rush after the ball.

In a spirit of fierce competition, the ski-resorts embarked upon a race at altitude. In 1984 Les Arcs opened an eighteen hole course at one thousand eight hundred and fifty metres above sea level. To outdo that achievement, Robert Berthet built the Flaine course at two thousand metres above sea level two years later. The record seemed unbeatable, but then 1993 saw it broken with the opening of the Tignes course at two thousand one hundred metres above sea level. The year after, Isola 2000 was built in the Alpes-Maritimes

The Grenoble-Bressom course at the foot of the Vercours appears to be in the middle of the countryside. The capital, Isère is, however, only a quarter of an hour away.

at the same altitude as Tignes. Since then, no courses have been built at altitude.

Near Grenoble, the courses are found at average altitudes. The highest point of Robert Trent Jones Junior's very beautiful course at Grenoble-Bresson is at four hundred metres above sea level. But from the top of its fairways, you play facing the Belledone, Chartreuse and Vercors mountain ranges. On the ninth hole, a descending par five, Grenoble is visible through a large break in the trees, which adds excitement to the second shot towards the green.

Architects do not necessarily need the beauty of the mountains for their imagination to have free rein. In Saint-Etienne, Thierry Sprecher transformed a

- 70 -

rubbish tip into a green oasis in the heart of the old mining town. "When I was brought to the site, it was full of stones, dogs were barking madly, it really was a dump," says the architect. As the history of the working classes is part of Saint-Etienne's heritage, a stele has been erected behind the putting green of the second hole as a memorial to the hundred miners who were killed in a firedamp explosion in the Chana shaft in 1942. The green is at the entry to the shaft, closing the final page of a dismal history.

In Lyons, the capital of the Gauls, the Villette d'Anthon course pioneered golf in the Rhône department. Built in 1965 on two hundred hectares along the river, the two courses designed by Hugues Lambert are a homage to different types of wild game. The championship course Les Sangliers (the Wild Boars) has back-tees which are unusually long at six thousand seven hundred and twenty seven metres. It was the site of the French Open in 1979 and the Lyons Open until 1994. The second eighteen holes are called Les Brocards (the Brockets) after the one year old kid goats who frolic with their mothers in the undergrowth. These two courses with their many water hazards are also home to wild swans, grey heron, egrets and black kite. A veritable Noah's Ark, a

Maison Blanche looks flat, but the undulating holes of the return stretch correct this impression.

The most photographed par three in Evian. The drive towards the green goes over a road and the players falls to daydreaming in admiration of Lake Geneva.

Divonne is one of France's most unusual golf courses. Its eighteen holes divide equally into par threes, par fours and par fives.
△

At the Royal Club Evian, the Alps are so near ... yet so far.
◁

Preceding pages:
At the weekend, the Swiss cross the border to try their luck on the well-protected greens of Maison Blanche.
◁◁

few kilometres away from the notorious Lyons traffic jams.

Less than three hours' drive from the Mediterranean coast and Italy, two hours from Switzerland and one hour away from the ski-resorts, France's third city enjoys a privileged position. At the weekends, the inhabitants of Lyons have a dazzling array of alternatives on offer. In the area near the Swiss border, golf courses are proliferating and, come the weekend, the inhabitants of Lyons find people from Geneva there, who only have to make a short trip across the border. Maison-Blanche, Esery, Bossey and Evian are the favourite courses of the Swiss and the inhabitants of the Rhône department. But Evian leads its competitors, because this town on the shores of Lake Geneva also has a casino for those who enjoy playing on green baize and two international class hotels, the Royal, a luxury hotel open since 1909 and the Hermitage, which offers Savoy charm. At the beginning of the century the grand reception rooms of the Royal were thronged with the celebrities of the day. On the Lake Geneva promenade, Isadora Duncan, Countess Anna de Noailles and the Princess of Hohenlohe showed off their gowns, while the princes, maharajahs and financial barons conversed over a cigar in the smoking room. With price no object, the Aga Khan reserved the hotel's finest suite in the western wing of the Royal. For more than forty years the spiritual head of the Ishmailis could be seen at Evian's evening receptions and in the afternoons on the golf courses, the first of which dates back to 1904.

This eighteen-hole course on Lake Geneva was rustic in style. At that time, modern standards were still far in the future. It was not until the renovation undertaken by Robert Trent Jones's former associate, Cabell Robinson, between 1988 and 1990, that the Royal Club Evian reached the level of quality demanded by the clients of the two great hotels. Then, on the initiative of the Danone Group, the owner of the luxury amenities in this Savoy town on Lake Geneva, an important ladies' event was created in 1994, the Evian Masters.

In the summer the resort of Gets is a favourite spot for hikers and golfers, who have only four months to enjoy this Alpine course.

Thanks to the dynamism of Antoine Ribaud and then his son Frank, the tournament has become one of the musts on the ladies' European circuit. Since the tournament's inauguration, the prize money has soared, and the course has recently been adorned with waterfalls and streams to bring out the elegant contours of these beautiful greens. During the four days of competition, these young ladies are treated like queens, just as Isadora Duncan or the poetess Anna de Noailles, Gabriele d'Annunzio's companion, were in their time. Whether on the lascivious fairways of Mâcon-la-Salle or at the Gala dinner for the lady champions of Evian, the story being written is that of the eternal feminine - a subject of delicacy and rounded contours.

At the foot of the Salève, a mountain overlooking Geneva, Robert Trent Jones has designed a highly technical course with long par threes and eighty-two bunkers !

The East

On the Eastern Borders

The East

In the course of the last century, the border from Strasbourg to Lons-le-Saunier was a constant source of dispute. Today the golf courses, much prized also by the Swiss and the Germans, symbolise a reconciliation which at one time would have been considered impossible. And the golf balls that whistle past are meant peaceably.

The flowery balconies, half-timbers and turrets of Alsatian houses.

△

Soufflenheim's fairways will end up being surrounded by houses, a pity!

◁

Preceding pages: The red sandstone castle of Haut Königsberg perches five hundred metres above sea-level. An impregnable fortress !

◁◁

Strasbourg, the capital of Europe, is quite a symbol. Pillaged, bombed, martyred, this magnificent town on the Rhine and the Ill was, on three occasions in seventy-five years, the justification behind the start of a terribly bloody war - in 1870, 1914 and 1940 – three black dates in France's history. This was quite a destiny for a city that had been declared a free town of the Germanic Empire in 1201, then annexed by Louis XIV in 1681, before being coveted by the German army in the nineteenth century and then serving as patriotic inspiration for the soldiers of the French army in August 1914.

It was against this bellicose background that golf in Alsace was established with the founding of Strasbourg-Illkirch in 1934, the same year in which the noise of Hitler's jackboots was resonating in Europe's ears.

At the beginning of the 60's, the reconciliation advocated by General de Gaulle and Chancellor Adenauer drew a line once and for all under almost a century of military rivalry. At the Rhin-Chalampé club, built on an island in the Rhine between Colmar and Mulhouse, Franco-German friendship has being going strong for thirty years. Thirty-three per cent of the members are French, German and Swiss respectively. A perfect ratio which is not enshrined in the club statutes. It is a rule that has been followed since the club opened in 1968 under the guidance of its Presidents and stewards, who are, however, always French.

This mix is a trademark of all the border golf clubs, from Soufflenheim, Bernhard Langer's latest creation, to Lons-le-Saulnier in the Jura. In Germany and Switzerland the construction of new courses is curbed by tighter environmental laws than in France. This has led to an input of capital from

At the Soufflenheim clubhouse, German is the first language. The border is a stone's throw away.
▷

Soufflenheim is the latest creation of the German champion, Bernhard Langer.
▽

German and Swiss financiers, which has given a significant boost to golf in the east of France.

Three national days of celebration are held in Rhin-Chalampé : the fourteenth of July for the French, the third of October for the Germans and the first of October for the Swiss. The clubhouse restaurant is draped in the appropriate national flags and everyone enjoys themselves. To complete this European round-up, England is represented by the course architect, David Harradine. On this island which is, from time to time, churned up by herds of wild boar, he has laid out an extremely classical course. At Rhin-Chalampé, oaks, poplars and birch are the main obstacles of this very long, narrow course with its back-tees. At six thousand four hundred metres it is one of the longest in France and breaking par requires quite some skill.

Rhin-Chalampé, one of France's longest courses, has straight, flat fairways, but is nevertheless difficult to score well on. △

The promoters of Kempferhof invited the American Robert Van Hagge to design their course whilst playing at Les Bordes.
△/▽

Arriving via the Plobsheim road to the Kempferhof golf course one has an immediate presentiment of the fate awaiting the golf balls. From the brackish water of the water hazards guarding the shared green of the ninth and eighteenth holes, it is clear that the architect, Robert Van Hagge, has stayed true to form and not skimped on traps for the golfers. It is a game of cat and mouse, with which the afficionados of the Seignosse, Les Bordes and Courson courses, Van Hagge's other creations, will be familiar. He has a predilection for undulating fairways, huge bunkers and island greens. They are his signature. One is never likely to get bored on his courses. The player must have technique, lucidity, strategy and not a little luck to pull off a good scorecard – a stark contrast to the more classical design of the Strasbourg Illkirch course.

The Kempferhof was conceived by three Alsatian promoters who wanted to bring a top of the range golf course to Strasbourg whilst they were cruising around Corsica in the middle of the Mediterranean. Their reference point was Les Bordes, Baron Marcel Michel's extraordinary course in the middle of the Sologne forest. When Robert Van Hagge was came into the picture, his creative genius was given carte blanche on a wooded estate around a hunting lodge.

The nineteenth-century hunting lodge facing a small chapel has become a charming hotel dedicated to the cinema. The décor of each of the thirteen rooms takes as its theme a masterpiece of the big screen, Jean-Luc Godard's La Chinoise, David Lean's Lawrence of Arabia, Max Ophül's Lola Montès ...not to mention the most splendid, the Eric von Stroheim Suite, a homage to the American producer and actor, whose performance as a German officer in Jean Renoir's La Grande Illusion has left its mark on generations of cinema-goers.

Those interested in fine food would prefer La Wantzeneau. This little village on the Ill, twelve kilometres to the north-east of Strasbourg is famous for its speciality restaurants. Sauerkraut, stuffed carp, trout, Riesling Chicken ... The most popular, A La Barrière, offers warm goose liver and pear stewed in Gewürztraminer. Gourmets would sell their souls for it. With such gastronomical delights on offer, it is advisable to visit La Wantzeneau golf course and

This par three at Kemperhof bears a strange resemblance to the second hole of the Golf National. The same green protected by a large water hazard – the same punishment.
△

Behind another Kemperhof par three, the hunting lodge has been converted into a hotel dedicated to the art of cinema.
◁

Following pages:
The Kempferhof is the best golfing challenge in Alsace. Although a sign on the road says there are twenty-seven holes, there are still only eighteen in the Plobsheim municipality.
▷▷

The La Largue golf course, a favourite of the Swiss, is a pastoral symphony. ▽

its Alsatian clubhouse with its geranium-decorated balconies before the clock strikes midday. The course, designed by the great Basque champion, Jean Garaialde, is regaled with water hazards. Built on the Ried, the former bed of the River Rhine, seven hectares of La Wantzeneau course's surface area is covered with water. This accounts for about ten per cent of the estate's area, a part of which is the site of some very modern residences - an Alsatian Florida. The role of the alligators is played by majestic white storks, which nest on top of the chimney stacks in the summer.

◁ La Wantzeneau's buildings were built after a model of an Alsatian village. The many water hazards point to its Floridian origins.

La Wantzeneau is an aquatic interlude before taking the wine road to Thann. Gewürztraminer, Riesling, Sylvaner, Tokay … fruity wines appreciated on both sides of the border. The road winds between hill-side vineyards and villages huddled around churches with slender steeples, climbing up to the impregnable fortress of Haut-Königsberg. It was in this former castle of Frederick Barbarossa, rebuilt by the German Emperor Wilhelm II, that Eric Von Stroheim gave his magisterial performance in La Grande Illusion, and which sixty years later led to the most beautiful suite in the Kempferhof hotel being named in his honour.

On these sloping greens the putter takes his shot with his back to the pretty village of Ammerschwihr.

△

In this pastoral landscape, where vineyards fight for space with the deep forests populated by wild boar, the golf club of Ammerschwihr follows the contours of the steep land at the foot of the Vosges. This is a proper mountain club which reaches four hundred metres above sea level. It is an exhausting climb to the greens set high above, but the views reward, plunging down towards the village of Ammerschwihr with its red-tiled roofs.

The department of La Franche-Comté also has a border with Switzerland. But in contrast to a golf club such as La Largue, the Doubs and Jura courses were set up by capital that was entirely French and mainly from big local firms.

The Ammerschwihr hills are covered in vineyards. After eighteen holes, a glass of white wine goes down well on the clubhouse terrace.

Such a course is the Prunevelle club near Sochaux, which was founded by the car company Peugeot's president, Jean-Pieree Peugeot, in 1928. He had already established the Sochaux football club whose hey-day was in the 30's, when, in their old Bonal stadium they won the French First Division Championship in 1935 and 1938, and the French Cup in 1937. In bringing golf to the factory-workers, he was revolutionary for the time. The first corporate golf course was seen in the Doubs. The Prunevelle course, in a golfing landscape that has since considerably changed, is still the only company golf course.

And yet other heads of small and medium-sized companies have since acquired golf courses, but not with the same social aim as the Peugeot family had in the pre-war period.

In the Jura, Christian de Grivel, chairman and managing director of V33, French market leader in wood varnishes, has saved nine country holes that were set to lie fallow. This sixty year old with red, dishevelled hair knows this little Lons-de-Saunier course. He came to play there, as he lived nearby. Like all good businessmen, he carried out an audit on the course, did some

number-crunching, looking to see what the possible return on his investment might be. Convinced of the viability of the project, he bought the club, contacted architect Hugues Lambert, who mapped the eighteen holes out for him on the corner of a tablecloth, and had a hotel built with thirty-six rooms and a restaurant. Christian de Grivel does not let the grass grow under his feet. A few years later his club officially known as "Le Val de Sorne" was transformed. A keen botanist, the owner has planted new trees, maples, oaks and despite them causing havoc to play, preserved some beautiful existing specimens. So a splendid ash tree nicknamed "the President's tree" stands plumb in the middle of fairway thirteen concealing from view an elevated green, which the golfers call "the Volcano".

The next hole which finishes at three hundred metres above sea level allows the remoteness, with the dead-end valleys typical of the Jura and the pretty villages of Vernantois, Moiron and Courbazon, to be taken in at a single glance. The fourteenth hole takes its name "the four belltowers" from a fourth village, Montaigu, into which its putting green extends, and where in 1760 Claude Roget de Lisle was born, composer of the Marseillaise, initially known as the Rhine army's war song.

The perfectly protected eighteenth green at the foot of the imposing La Largue clubhouse.
▷

Saved from bankruptcy by an industrialist passionate about golf, Val De Sorne is today one of the " musts " in the Jura.
△

Often, wars which are remembered in an excess of pride as victories are in fact shameful defeats, pitiful skirmishes. At the Besançon golf club, set in a very pretty pine forest, the players easily under-estimate these eighteen holes, which appear – the illusion dear to golfers - easy. After negotiating with greater or lesser success, the first fifteen holes, fatigue, weariness and pressure begin to take their toll. The sixteenth hole is a rather unexciting par five, straight as a die to four hundred and eighty two metres, but the drive

has to make it down a narrow corridor edged with shrubbery. Without fail the golf trollies are to be found near the trees, whilst their owners pull apart branches looking for their golf balls. The winning scorecard that one was proudly expecting to show off to friends on the clubhouse terrace metamorphoses into a chit of paper that is shamefacedly signed upon leaving the eighteenth green. This cursed hole has inspired members to form a club association named "the sixteen at sixteen". Sixteen strokes – yes, you have read correctly – on the par five of hole sixteen. "All the Besançon golfers are members" they declare with a guffaw. After so many testing times throughout history, the people of Eastern France have learnt to laugh at adversity.

At Val de Sorne, more generally known as the Lons-le-Saunier course, the hotel rooms look out over the fairways. Silence is guaranteed !

From One Renaissance to Another

On the Banks of the Loire

From Sologne to Touraine the banks of the Loire are a wonderful open-air museum of the Renaissance. Each château rivals the last in beauty and architectural audacity and in the heart of the these forests which abound in wild game nestles Les Bordes, one of the most beautiful golf courses in France. It is a masterpiece which stands comparison with Chambord, the hunting lodge of François I.

At Orléans-Limière, the reception is housed in a glass tower. △

From Les Bordes' first hole, the surroundings are well-established. The greens are the targets and the bunkers veritable strands. ◁

Cabell Robinson, former assistant of the inspirational Robert Trent Jones, poses on Orléans-Limère's fairways with its indented greens. ▷

Preceding pages: Catherine de Medici, Diane de Poitiers and Madame de Staël all stayed in the Chaumont-sur-Loire castle. ◁◁

From Orléans to Saumur, the Loire valley is known as the Valley of the Kings. Since the Capetian dynasty up until François I, it was the residence of the French kings. In this region of forests and lakes, rich in wild game, Italian architects outdid each other's creative genius to build castles and hunting lodges. Even when the King and his court chose Paris as the capital city, the building of these princely domains overlooking the Loire did not end. In the nineteenth century it was the middle-class who vied with each other in the neo-gothic and neo-classical architecture of their residences deep in the heart of Sologne.

This cradle of the Renaissance, the Valley of the Kings, which attracted the greatest foreign craftsmen of the fifteenth and sixteenth centuries, was able to lure the biggest names in English and American golfing architecture in the

Orléans-Limière, designed by Cabell Robinson, is the entry point for the golf courses built on the grounds of the Loire châteaux. △

Near Les Bordes, Jim Shirley built a more modest course at Prieuré de Ganay where the bunkers are replaced by grassy depressions. △

twentieth. Cabell Robinson at Orléans-Limère, Michael Fenn at Touraine and master of them all, Robert Van Hagge at Les Bordes.

The Peugeot Golf Guide, a reference guide for the grading of European golf clubs, gave Les Bordes nineteen out of twenty in its 1998 edition. This exceptional course in the heart of La Sologne shares this honour with sixteen other, long revered golf course masterpieces, Valderrama in Spain, Royal County Down and Royal Portrush in Northern Ireland, Muirfield and Carnoustie in Scotland, Royal Birkdale and Royal Lytham St. Anne's in England, clubs who have hosted prestigious tournaments such as the British Open, the Ryder Cup, the Walker Cup. Les Bordes, however, is an exception. In keeping with the wishes of Baron Marcel Bich, who made his fortune by

Les Bordes : Baron Bich wanted an international class golf course and Robert Van Hagge produced this for him. On the fearsome Loir-et-Cher course, the bunkers are as large as the fairways, there are island greens and the clubhouse, despite its apparent simplicity, is extremely comfortable.

◁
◁/▽

inventing the ball-point pen sold under his name, and those of his associate, the Japanese, M. Sakuraï, this championship course with its fearsome reputation only welcomes "Sunday" players to do battle with the monster. A pity, because with its six thousand four hundred and twelve metres of back tees it would be a tremendous test for the professionals.

Les Bordes has generated respect since it opened in 1987. Those walking its fairways admire it and those dreaming of rising to its challenge fear it. Today, however, the difficulty of the course has been moderated, by clearing some of the undergrowth and re-modelling teeing grounds making it more

have attracted golfers from Loire-et-Cher and Parisians who come to practice their follow-through before squaring up to the monster next door. This twenty-seven-hole course, which is to be extended to thirty-six holes in the year 2000, was designed for Baron Bich by Robert Van Hagge's associate, Jim Shirley. It was the philosophy of this American pro, who has lived in France for fourteen years, that attracted the Baron : "Golf should be fun, fast and easy to play." The antithesis of Van Hagge. The task set by the Baron seemed impossible : a course which everyone could play on, which does not lose too many balls, whose building and maintenance costs are kept to the bare minimum. Jim Shirley received three million francs for a nine-hole section. It was not much, but enough for the Texan. With wisdom far beyond his years, he built the first section, the red, in the style of a links. Then he turned his attention to the blue section, nine holes amid the birch trees, and then the yellow, a mix of the first two courses. The last, which is due to open in the autumn, winds through oak woods. In Prieuré de Ganay the sandwedge can be left in the boot of the car, for the twenty-seven holes only have sixteen bunkers ! A record. On the red course, you have to wait until the fifth hole to be faced with even a trace of sand. "The approaches to the greens have been shaped as light grassy depressions which one day could be filled with sand" the architect explains. In order to compensate for the lack of hazards, the greens are small, irregularly-shaped and elevated. "The best in the area," insist the habitués, enabling Prieuré de Ganay to defend its par thirty-six on each nine holes with pride.

Sept Tours castle is these days a hotel and the chapel has been converted into a clubhouse.
▽

Tours-Ardrée is one of the two courses in the Centre region and part of the Blue Green chain. ▷

approachable. At Les Bordes, even remaining at par is a worthy score, not to mention a birdie ! Regular players say that the trick is to play each hole as a bogey, a defensive strategy which rules out playing each green by the book, in the hope of achieving the impossible.

For in this hunting region, birdies and eagles flee at the first drive like a deer tracked by a pack of dogs. The golfers usually come back empty-handed, game bag empty of triumphant scores, their follow-through in disarray and their hearts heavy. In Les Bordes pride comes before a fall at the water hazards and the lesson learnt is one of humility.

When the course opened, golfers discovered the work of a golf architect then unknown in France, Robert Van Hagge. He has since built golf courses all over mainland France, Seignosse, Kempferhof, Courson-Monteloup, Golf National ... They are unanimously agreed to be great courses, even though some complain that the design is a little too complex and that they are expensive to maintain.

Free from illusions about the quality of French golfers, Baron Marcel Bich decided a few years later to build another course next to Les Bordes, a golf course that would be easy to play and within everyone's budget. Six years after opening, Prieuré de Ganay is still keeping its side of the bargain. The yearly membership fee of four thousand francs, green-fees of one hundred francs during the week and one hundred and forty francs at the weekend

In the shadow of the crenellated towers of Sept Tours castle, Michael Fenn's wide course means that the driver can be used safely.
◁

At the castle one dines in fine style. This is French-style bourgeois chic.
▽

At Sept Tours castle, the course is well-watered ...
◁

◁◁ *Double preceding page In the heart of the Sologne forest, Les Bordes unfolds its perfectly-maintained fairways.*

have attracted golfers from Loire-et-Cher and Parisians who come to practice their follow-through before squaring up to the monster next door. This twenty-seven-hole course, which is to be extended to thirty-six holes in the year 2000, was designed for Baron Bich by Robert Van Hagge's associate, Jim Shirley. It was the philosophy of this American pro, who has lived in France for fourteen years, that attracted the Baron : "Golf should be fun, fast and easy to play." The antithesis of Van Hagge. The task set by the Baron seemed impossible : a course which everyone could play on, which does not lose too many balls, whose building and maintenance costs are kept to the bare minimum. Jim Shirley received three million francs for a nine-hole section. It was not much, but enough for the Texan. With wisdom far beyond his years, he built the first section, the red, in the style of a links. Then he turned his attention to the blue section, nine holes amid the birch trees, and then the yellow, a mix of the first two courses. The last, which is due to open in the autumn, winds through oak woods. In Prieuré de Ganay the sandwedge can be left in the boot of the car, for the twenty-seven holes only have sixteen bunkers ! A record. On the red course, you have to wait until the fifth hole to be faced with even a trace of sand. "The approaches to the greens have been shaped as light grassy depressions which one day could be filled with sand" the architect explains. In order to compensate for the lack of hazards, the greens are small, irregularly-shaped and elevated. "The best in the area," insist the habitués, enabling Prieuré de Ganay to defend its par thirty-six on each nine holes with pride.

Sept Tours castle is these days a hotel and the chapel has been converted into a clubhouse.
▽

Tours-Ardrée is one of the two courses in the Centre region and part of the Blue Green chain. ▷

Following the Loire from Chambord to Tours the towers of the Renaissance castles can be seen rising up from around the meanders of the longest river in France. Amboise, Chaumont-sur-Loire, Chenonceaux, Azay-le-Rideau ... Given today's astronomical maintenance costs, very few of these castles with their Italian architecture are still used as private residences, so families anxious to preserve the family heritage open the castles to visitors for a few hours each day. At the Cheverny castle, the Marquis Charles Antoine de Sigalas Hurault de Vibray devotes much energy to keeping up the estate, in the family for five centuries. Son et Lumière shows, hunting, public access to the castle (Cheverny was the first castle to open its doors to the public in 1922) allow the Marquis to keep up the estates. Many Tintin fans also make the pilgrimage to Cheverny, the vast residence finished in 1634, which was used by Tintin's creator Hergé as the model for Moulinsart, Captain Haddock's castle.

Don't imagine yourself dining at the manor; it is not part of the Tours-Ardrée course.

- 105 -

The golf course which opens out on the land opposite the castle is another source of revenue for the Marquis. The eighteen holes around La Rousselière, a forty-two hectare lake, do not however have a view onto the castle. Bearing in mind what a trump card it would be to have fairways rolling up to this "princely domain", the Taiwanese owners are planning to extend the course. This plan should inspire the Tintin fans, dressed in golf breeches like their hero. And to the delight of cartoon fans, all types of Milou are allowed onto the course.

The golf courses of Tours, however, have made the castles part of the site. On the Ardrée course a pretty manorhouse, still lived in, is one of the jewels in the crown of the Blue Green chain, a castle-hotel with seven neo-gothic towers on a course of the same name, around which lies a very flat golf course of questionable golfing interest. On the Touraine course stands a beautiful nineteenth century bourgeois residence which looks onto a splendid and magnificently wooded course.

In 1973 the golfers of the region, driven out by the building of a new motorway, moved across to Ballan-Miré on the La Touche estate and built the Touraine course. On a limited area, the English architect, Michael Fenn, designed eighteen holes in the form of a snail, whilst still retaining the land's magnificent trees – peduncle oaks, white poplars, sequoias, Judea trees, junipers, Algerian pines … a paradise for budding botanists who take the opportunity to admire, before driving the par three of the sixteenth hole, the majestic five hundred year old oak which stretches out its imposing branches on the left of the teeing ground.

In this welcoming private club, children rule the roost. On Sundays they crowd onto the eight hundred square metres of putting green on the site of an old kitchen garden for chip and put competitions. This fun-filled training has paid off for the Touraine club, which carried off the French Club Championship, stealing the crown of the Racing Club of France and its star teams. A far cry from the showiness of the Parisian clubs, it is the Sébastian Van Doorens and Julien van Hauwes of the Touraine club who represent the future, if not the Renaissance, of French golf.

The Touraine golf club was founded in 1973 on the La Touche estate. Botanists enjoy this course which has pre-served its ancient trees.

Ile de France

*I*n Capital Letters

Ile de France

Ile de France is the region of France which boasts the most golf courses. No surprise given that it is also the most populated area. The sport really took off in the 1980's when the middle classes started to play golf. The golf enthusiast has a huge array of choices on offer from big private clubs to commercial ones.

The Saint-Nom-La-Bretèche clubhouse was a farm under Louis XIV. △

The very pretty par three at Saint-Nom-la-Bretèche. Just an eight or nine iron is enough to try a birdy. ◁

The first hole of the red and the blue courses opens out from the flowery putting-green of Saint-Nom-La-Bretèche. ▷

Preceding pages: The Palace of Versailles was the residence of Louis XIV, the Sun King. Today it is the most visited palace in France. ◁◁

Fortune has smiled on the Parisians, giving them a whole range of courses to choose from, for seven of the eight departments of the region (Seine-et-Marne, Yvelines, Essonne, Hauts-de-Seine, Seine-Saint-Denis, Val de Marne and Val de Oise) offer seventy courses for golfers to gorge themselves on. This figure easily swells if the courses south of the Oise are counted, which are less than forty kilometres from the Paris ring road. Moreover, it is the people of the Ile de France who account for the largest single group of golfers (ninety thousand out of two hundred and ninety thousand), about a

The little islet on the right is the dropping-zone for two adjacent holes of Saint-Nom-La-Bretèche.
▷

A water hazard was added to the green of this par four at Saint-Nom-La-Bretèche for the Lancôme Trophy event.
▽

third, registered by the French Golfing Federation. It is against this background that the commercial courses have embarked upon a considerable price war. There are Senior Citizens' days, Ladies' days, green-fees which include a meal ... golf club stewards have stretched their imagination to find ways of attracting this new custom. The private clubs, however, long kept their doors closed to avoid being swamped by a rush of new arrivals, until they too were caught up in the prevailing trend and had to lower their entry requirements to make up for the loss of members lured away by the modern layouts and lower membership fees of these new clubs.

If you wish to play golf in the Paris region, it is better to live in the west than in the north-east. For Yvelines, which is home to more golfers than anywhere else in France, (almost twenty three thousand) is also the

The view from the elevated third hole at Fontainebleau takes in France's largest forest.
△

department with the most courses. It has twenty-two compared to one in Seine-Saint-Denis ! And double compared to the Val d'Oise. This inequality can be traced back to the social make-up, which has prevailed since the last century, of a more industrialised eastern Paris and a more middle-class and leisured west. Golf in the Paris region has also developed in the less populated parts of the Ile de France. This is why the agricultural areas of the southern part of Essonne and the western part of Seine-et-Marne have also been caught up in the golfing frenzy. At the same time, the small department of Hauts-de-Seine did not have the necessary space to build eighteen-hole golfing facilities, not to mention the dizzying level of land prices. This department has just one course of over nine holes, the very private Saint-Cloud course. Today, it is still the nearest course (it has thirty-six holes) to the capital, less than eight kilometres to the porte Maillot. Built on land of the Buzenval castle, battlefield of the French and the Prussians on 19th January 1871, the Saint-Cloud course boasts the amusing feature of not having a single square metre in the municipality of the same name. It was, however, the opening of the the Saint Cloud Country Club on December 6th 1911 which gave the club, whose fairways extend into the municipalities of Garches and Vaucresson, its name. Its location so close

The Morfontaine coat of arms is that of the most exclusive club in France. △
The International Club of Lys is a family club with many sports on offer, two eighteen-hole golf courses, a pool, a tennis court and a riding stables.
◁

The Chantilly clubhouse, French counterpart of the Royal and Ancient at St. Andrew's.
▽

to Paris is an immense advantage for the club, which has welcomed crowned heads of state such as the Duke of Windsor, Léopold of Belgium and King Hassan II as well as political figures such as Dwight Eisenhower and President Mittérand, who liked to come for his weekly match on Mondays, when the club was closed.

Although the Paris region is today at the forefront of French golf, it took decades for the sport to become established, because the first courses, still exciting today, were not laid out until the beginning of the twentieth century, about fifty years after the Pau course had opened. The turn of the century saw a revolution in French golf as it changed from a holiday sport played on the Riviera, or on the Basque and Norman coasts, into a weekend hobby, if not indeed a daily one.

Three great courses were opened in the years 1900 to 1910 : La Boulie in 1901, Fontainebleau in 1908 and Chantilly the year after. The first, La Boulie, enjoyed the privilege of calling itself "The Paris Golf Club" before it became The Racing Club of France, La Boulie. Since then, two clubs have dared to use the name of the capital in their titles : The Paris International Golf Club at Bouffémont and the nine holes of the Saint-Cloud hippodrome, the Paris Country Club.

Fontainebleau's club-house bar and frescoes by Paul Tavernier.
▽

Of this trio, it is Chantilly which remains closest to tradition. Five of its members are in the Royal and Ancient of St. Andrews, the guardian of golfing orthodoxy. At the Chantilly club, sponsors are kindly requested to keep their distance. The Sunday competitions are financed by the members

Sandstone rocks bar the access to the splendid par five of Fontainebleau's twelfth hole. ▷

and the silver cups and plates are a worthy substitute for the logo-covered umbrellas, towels and pullovers that mark the prize-giving ceremonies of the commercial clubs. "We are amongst gentlemen, let us therefore behave like gentlemen," is the maxim of these golfers of another era, who delight in playing the two eighteen-hole courses, Le Vineuil, the original course, and Les Longères.

Opened on the 28th of September 1909 with an exhibition match between the two great champions of the era, Arnaud Massy and Jean Gassiat, the club has hosted ten French Opens and all the big amateur events. The world's best players, including Bobby Jones, have come to square up to the Le Vineuil course's six thousand five hundred and ninety seven metres, a masterpiece of intelligent architecture by the Englishman Tom Simpson, and everyone has suffered on the terrible roughs reminiscent of those in the British Open.

The Saint Germain clubhouse restored after the terrible fire of 29th December 1952.

The Saint-Germain honours board with the name of Severiano Ballesteros, who recorded the course's best score of sixty-two.

At Fontainebleau, there is hardly any rough to speak of, but it is as well to be aware that wayward golf balls are likely to end up in the dense forest, whose rocks and undergrowth tightly hug the fairways. The forest's famous sandstone rocks are sometimes integrated into the course, as on the twelfth hole, a long, rising par five, two thirds of which is blocked by white rocks which look like foam-covered waves rolling on a grassy ocean. For about sixty years, new golf clubs opened as slowly as a new player makes progress : Port-Marly, now gone, Saint-Germain, Morfontaine, the most exclusive club in France, International Club du Lys and Saint-Nom-la-Bretèche, which at the end of the fifties was the first example of a French-style golf property. Thanks to the Lancôme trophy event which has been played here since 1970, the thirty-six hole Saint-Nom-La-Brèteche course has become an international venue.

RECORDS DU PARCOURS		
PROFESSIONNELS		
1936	H. COTTON	65
1949	U. GRAPPASONNI	65
1952	A.D. LOCKE	64
1958	P. THOMSON	64
1965	J. GARAIALDE	64
1985	S. LYLE	63
1985	S. BALLESTEROS	62
AMATEURS		
1959	H. DE LAMAZET	68
1992	A. VALENZUELA	67
1992	J. SPENCER	64

It was the 1970's and the 1980's that saw the Ile de France becoming dotted with little red flagsticks. This time, as golf took off in France, it was the Paris region that was in the vanguard. Especially since the first public

golf course had been opened at Saint-Aubin on August 15th 1974 thanks to the efforts of two idealists, Emmanuel Veillas and Gilles Boutrolle, who were to make a great contribution to the golf explosion of the 80's through their company SOGEL (Société de gestion d'équipement de loisirs). The percentage of registered golfers was to increase by more than twenty per cent a year during these years of plenty. It was a golden age. From now on, golf was to be a sport open to the middle classes. These new players wanted to be able to play immediately and cheaply. Gone were the never-ending practice sessions under the finicky eye of the golf instructors. The golf clubs turned a blind eye to atypical swings and money rolled into the coffers. The investors immediately followed suit and architects left their buildings to devote their full energies to designing fairways and greens. Projects poured in and the designers worked night and day to meet the demand. It was also at this time that the Japanese made a dramatic appearance on the French golf scene, opening courses at Cély-en-Bière, Fontenailles, Clément-Ader, Feucherolles and Apremont, to name but a few.

A Japanese folly, Cély castle, was completely refurbished and its rooms decorated with great art.
◁

At Cély-en-Bière, the Urban Group spared no expense. Taking up an unfinished project, two French architects, Mark Adam and Patrick Fromanger, were instructed to build a new course entirely on sand. Waterfalls, great clumps of flowers, open-air sculpture adorn this garden course, which is so perfectly maintained that many players, unaccustomed to such magnificence, do not dare to strike their ball onto the fairway for fear of destroying this wall-enclosed paradise. The little castle has become the clubhouse and there are underground parking facilities. When the club opened, two hundred and fifty million francs had been spent ! For the grand opening, the golf promoters organised a World Ladies' Championship for the eight best lady professionals. Since then, the Urban Group has fallen into financial difficulty in Japan, and the club is now managed on a less lavish scale by Frenchmen.

The cosy interior of the Joyenval dining room, the latest exclusive club to be built near the capital.
▽

During this economic boom, American architects were much in demand. Their prestigious names ensured immediate publicity for the new courses. Jack Niklaus is the designer of the course at the Paris International Golf Club at Baillet-en-France, Robert Trent Jones Senior of the two eighteen-hole courses at Joyenval in the Retz desert, Ronald Fream at L'Isle-Adam and the Eurodisney course in the Brie plains and Robert Van Hagge of the twenty-seven holes of the Courson-Monteloup, and in collaboration with Hubert Chesneau, the general mana-

Feucherolles, designed by Jean-Marie Pellot, is regaled with water hazards. The Paris Saint-Germain football team can be seen on this very popular course during the week.

The ninth hole of the Albatross course with its narrow green fifty metres deep. ◁

The fourth hole of the Golf National's Albatross course has the appearance of an Irish links. ▽

above:
La Chouette castle's course was designed by Robert Trent Jones Junior. It will soon be extended to eighteen holes. △

Centre:
The Rebetz course in Oise is reputed, quite justifiably, to have the finest greens of the Paris region. Although the clubhouse is very welcoming, the castle behind the eighteenth hole is privately owned. No entry ! △

The private club of Prieuré to the west of Paris has two magnificent wooded eighteen-hole courses. ▷

twenty-four or below, the Albatross (the Golf National has another eighteen holes, the Eagle, and a nine-hole introductory course l'Oiselet) is the best test of golf in the Paris region. Playing to one's handicap requires either a miracle or an acute sense of strategy given the countless difficulties, which makes even the most solid swing falter. You do not go to the Golf National for the landscape – it holds no interest – nor for the clubhouse atmosphere which is reduced to the bare minimum, but for love of the game and to flirt with danger. You are strongly advised to bring along your shrimping net to fish the balls out of the water hazards which are scattered over eleven of the eighteen holes.

The Prieuré golf course takes its name from this magnificent building, now the clubhouse.

Today, Paris and the region around it lives off its past achievements. Only one course has opened in 1998, the La Chouette Golf course in Yvelines, designed by Robert Trent Jones, soon to be extended to eighteen holes. All that remains to do is to equip the Ile de France's departments which do not have many golfing facilities, such as Seine-Sainte-Denis, with some compact urban courses, the like of which can be seen in Rueil-Malmaison and L'Ile Fleurie, Chatou or Haras de Jardy in Vaucresson, and to build a proper practice ground in Paris on the Longchamp and Auteuil race courses, which are deserted apart from at race meetings. The plans are ready and waiting; they only have to be implemented for the words "Paris" and "golf" to be written in capital letters.

The Paris International Club in the Val d'Oise is the only course in France designed by Jack Nicklaus. For two years the women on the European circuit have played the Ladies' French Open there, suffering on the eighteenth island green which does not look kindly on attacks taken too timidly.

*T*he Northern Region

Four Authentic Links

France's golf links lie amongst high sand dunes and at a point within view of the English coastline. Every weekend, the British, armed with their golf clubs, cross the Channel for very "British" games of golf - in a wind that would delight any Scotsman.

At Le Touquet, the La Mer course lies in the dunes. It is a real links, resembling those found in Scotland. △

When the rough grows at Wimereux, the regulars nickname it "Wimerough". ◁

Preceding pages: A boat trip on the waterways and drainage works of Saint-Omer. ◁◁

From the roof of the blockhouse, now a back-tee of the twelfth hole of the Wimereux course, the coast of England is visible on the horizon only thirty kilometres away. It used to be that only the daily departing ferries plied the route between Calais and the English ports of Folkestone, Dover and Ramsgate. Now, tourists use the Channel Tunnel, a thirty kilometre passageway under the sea. These days France is only a two and a half hour journey from London. At weekends, the British come over to the continent to play on the great links of the Pas-de-Calais and the coast of Picardy, such as Wimereux, Le Touquet, Hardelot, Belle Dune. They come in couples or in all male groups and can be recognised by their wind-cheaters and quasi-uniform of woolly hats. This is a return to their roots for the English, who delight in these links built by their ancestors.

Whitley, Stoneham, Argyll : these subjects of the British Empire were not only golfers but also builders. Their fertile imagination transformed desolate landscape into fashionable sea-side resorts. At the end of the nineteenth century, Sir John Whitley discovered the sand dunes that stretch from Cap Gris Nez to the mouth of the Authie river. Enchanted by this wild, wind-battered landscape, this man of commerce set about creating a fully-fledged town that he wished to christen Mayville, a Franco-English name in honour of Princess May de Teck, the future wife of George V, who was to reign over Great Britain and the Indian Empire from 1910 to 1936. This rather hare-brained project was to come to nothing. At the same time, in association with another Englishman, Allan Stoneham, he set up the Touquet Syndicate Ltd. and, in his gaiters, walked the length of the coast looking for the ideal site.

The La Mer du Touquet course is the English golfer's favourite French links. Here, they feel at home.

About thirty kilometres north of Le Touquet he came upon a charming castle, updated to the purest neo-gothic style by Sir John Hare in 1849. This castle with its thirteenth century ramparts was to serve as the "foundation stone" of Hardelot-Plage, an internationally recognised seaside resort. One of its towers marks the first tee of the nine holes designed at the beginning of the century by the English champion, Harry Vardon, who won the British Open a record six times. There is hardly anything left of this rudimentary course. Only three holes of the present course at Les Pins, the thirteenth, fourteenth and sixteenth, can be traced back to the first golf course at Hardelot and a few yellowing photographs bring a touch of history to the green-papered walls of the clubhouse bar.

The Hardelot course, which had been extended to eighteen holes with Tom Simpson's marvellous design in 1930, could not stand up to the massive Allied air bombings whose mission was to destroy the second world war defences of the Germans. Hardelot-Plage was left in ruins. Only eight villas were left intact ! It was clear that rebuilding the golf course would not

be the top priority after the war and it was only possible to re-open it in 1953. A stroke of fortune meant that Tom Simpson's original design (he was also the architect of Chiberta, Chantilly and Fontainebleau) had been preserved. The Hardelot course lies in forest whose earliest trees took root at the time of Louis XIII and the course is straightforward even if its bunkers are judiciously placed. Tom Simpson was always fair in his designs and demands finesse and technique from golfers. The enthusiasm for golf on the "Opal Coast", (the name given to the stretch of coast between Berck and Cap Gris Nez by the painter Levêque at the beginning of the century) led the Lesur family, who has presided over the Hardelot-Plage's development and the destiny of golf for three generations, to open, in 1990, a new eighteen-hole course hidden amongst the dunes of Mount Saint Frieux at just over a kilometre from the first course. Designed by the Belgian, Paul Rollin, the eighteen holes of Les Dunes are more undulating, and plenty of doglegs and water hazards emphasise its modern style. Nonetheless, Les Dunes has been criticised by some French golfers for its several blind teeing grounds. This makes Ken Strachan start up from his manager's chair. The Scotsman

Tom Simpson, the English architect, has put his name to one of the most beautiful French courses, the Pins course, at Hardelot.

- 133 -

cites Gleneagles, Augusta, Lahinch. "Who criticises the blind holes of these legendary courses ? Did Tiger Woods complain about the blind drive at the eleventh hole of the Master's ?" The subject makes Ken Strachan, a former pro, bristle.

Come wind or rain, the British players never complain : they are only too happy to be playing another round with office colleagues. For the rain has never beaten one of Her Majesty's subjects nor a golfer from the Nord-Pas-de-Calais region. To the visiting Parisian who is already sagging under the yoke of a force three, one retorts that at Wimereux the game only starts to get interesting when you are bent double on the fairways and the umbrellas are turned inside out, their ribs broken. In any case Wimereux is not a proper golf course unless it is windy, say the members of this club, which is nearest in character to the leading Scottish clubs. It is pure, yet tough and when the rough grows, it becomes "Wimerough", a monster.

On the vast sandy beaches of Le Touquet the brightly-coloured speed-sails zoom by in the wind. At low tide, dare-devils sitting in their half-motor, half-

On the Dunes d'Hardelot course, some players grumble about the blind teeing grounds. Criticism which makes the steward leap up from his arm-chair. △

Inspired by Robert Trent Jones, the architect of Dunes d'Hardelot has enjoyed himself with the target greens. ▷

Dunes d'Hardelot was designed by the Belgian architect, Paul Rolin.

sailing boat contraptions have a playground stretching for kilometres. On the sandy tracks of the dunes, motorcycle riders step on the accelerator in preparation for the big annual race, the Le Touquet Enduro, which attracts hundreds of competitors from all over Europe. Amidst the dunes, peacable golfers try their luck on one of Frances's great and noble courses, the La Mer du Touquet golf club. "La Mer", however, is not Le Touquet's first course, as it did not open until 1931. Twenty-seven years earlier, Lord Balfour, the then British Prime Minister had opened the La Forêt course ! That was quite a coup. But then Le Touquet is no ordinary town : it was not founded until the end of the nineteenth century. The first houses were not built until 1882 and then hotels and shops followed. In 1888 Le Touquet assumed the title of "Paris Plage" (the Paris Strand), but, in spite of everything, the resort did not take off, so John Whitley (founder of Hardelot), with his associate Allen Stoneham, put in a bid for eleven hundred hectares of unsold land. The dynamism of these Englishmen was legendary.

Under their direction, a luxury hotel, casino, race course and golf course rose from the soil, or rather from the sand. Before the war, Le Touquet was the only French, indeed only continental European course to have forty-five holes. These club members are spoiled. Blessed be Stoneham ! His grateful family have erected a stele to the right of the eighteenth green of La Forêt in memorial of the great man, founder of the Le Touquet golf club.

During the Second World War two thousand bombs exploded on Le Touquet. After the town had been liberated on the 4th of September 1944, mine-clearing operations started. They were long, dangerous and laborious. The town was riddled with them. Those clearing the mines numbered one hundred thousand ! The golf course was gradually re-opened nine holes at a time. Acquired by the Open Golf Club chain, the course is now just as it was when it was laid out in 1931 by the English architect Harry Colt, the creator of the Saint-Cloud, Wentworth and Muirfield courses. A paradox of the course is that the sea is not visible from the fairways. Only at the

The wood, slate and bow-windows of the little Belle Dune clubhouse.
▷

The Belle Dune course is not long, but demands great precision with the irons on the second shots.
▽

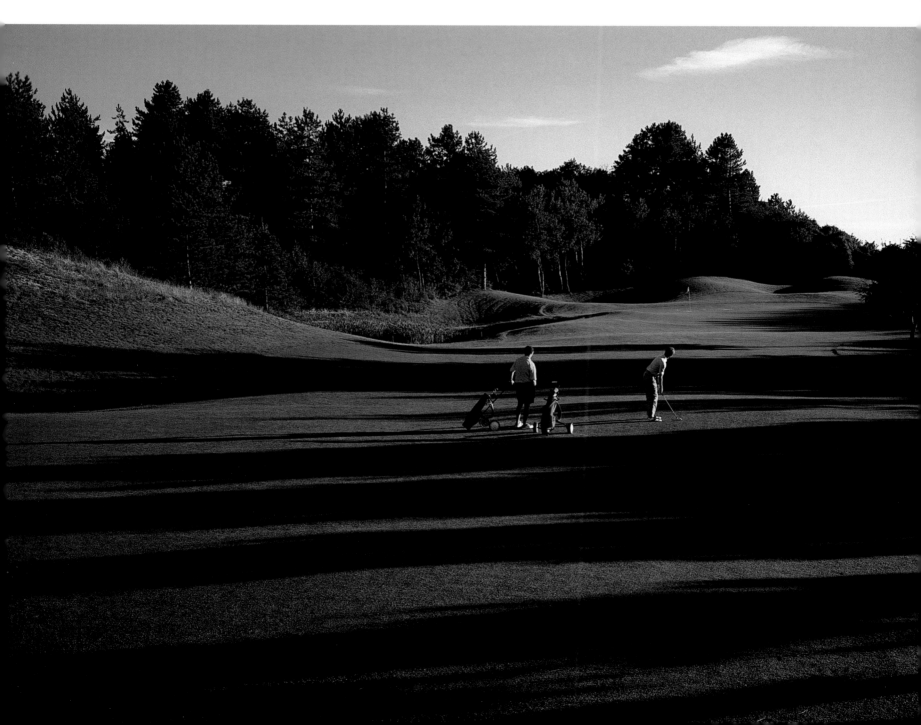

teeing ground of the eighteenth, turning one's back to the course, can the sea be glimpsed between two huge sand dunes covered in beach grass.

With the proliferation of American-style courses between 1985 to 1995, a golf architect could have considered building a links the ultimate exercise in nostalgia. For at that time, new golfers were demanding courses peppered with water hazards, island greens and bunkers as huge as a Breton inlet ! Two French architects, however, rose to the challenge. Yves Bureau at Saint-Jean-de-Monts in the Vendée and Jean-Manuel Rossi at Belle-Dune on the Picardy coast. Belle-Dune was hailed as one of the most beautiful French courses constructed in the 1990's. Built by the Syndicat de la Côte Picarde, the Belle-Dune course at Fort-Mahon-Plage exemplifies a successful union of golf and ecology. For it took two years of research to find solutions to the problems posed by building this course on the largest area of sand dunes in Europe. In order to keep the dunes in place, more than a million beach grass plants were planted by hand ; to stabilize the lawns, prepared earth was spread onto the sand and to guide the watering, a watertight film was placed forty centimetres below the ground. Belle-Dune has been monitored by researchers since it opened and only the rabbits who are culled every Friday during the winter months are not welcome in this environment.

In contrast to other links which may appear uninteresting, Belle-Dune beckons one to a three-part stroll. The first, between holes one to eleven, crosses a forest of pine and birch trees, the second, from the twelfth to the fourteenth hole, enters the sand dunes. There is a vivid contrast between these verdant greens and the thousands of yellowish beach grass plants undulating in the wind which surround them. Keeping environmental considerations in mind, Jean-Manuel Rossi has not baulked at separating holes twelve and thirteen by several hundred metres and has constructed wooden bridges in order to keep the natural environment intact. Along the final holes, from fifteen to eighteen, the pine trees return to border the fairways and run up to the clubhouse, a charming wooden building, whose slate roof and bow-windows emphasise its Picardy style.

Yet another golfing walk on which the sea is hidden from view, although it is only just over a kilometre away, just as in Le Touquet, Hardelot, Wimereux or the other great links across the Channel. As the sun sets, the English, surfeited with lawns and sand and dizzied by the wind, wend their way towards the Channel Tunnel.

Preceding pages:
Belle Dune's first holes wind through the forest before plunging into the largest area of sand dunes in Europe.
◁◁

Thousands of beach grass seedlings were planted to stabilise the high sand mounds on the Belle Dune course.
◁

Normandy

From Granville to Etretat

Normandy

Situated between sea and bocage landscape, the golf courses of Normandy have found a natural home on its soft, green meadows. From Granville to Etretat, the grass is lush and the rains coming in from the west make this region a green-keeper's paradise.

The Granville clubhouse, an example of typical Norman architecture. △

The lush and velvety Etretat greens against a backgound of white chalk cliffs. At Etretat, the golfer putts as the seagulls fly beneath.◁

Preceding pages:
The rocky islet of Mont Saint-Michel celebrated its thousandth anniversary in 1966. At high tide, the water comes in at the speed of a galloping horse.
◁◁

The three syllables Nor-man-dy conjure up a wealth of images : cider, apple-trees in blossom, dairy cattle, strong-smelling cheese and lush meadows. The grass is rich and verdant in this land stretching from the Dieppe cliffs to Mont Saint-Michel and lapped by the temperate waters of the English Channel. Golf courses have found natural sanctuary on these pastures. There is no need for fertilisers here and the rains carried by the west wind make the grass on the courses grow like wildfire.

Golf has weighed anchor on the shoreline, along the vast sandy beaches of Granville or atop the high, white limestone cliffs of Dieppe and Etretat. The development of golf in Normandy followed the fashions in seaside resorts where rich Parisians took their holidays – Dieppe, Etretat, Cabourg, Granville and then Deauville, the small town in Calvados, seen rather grandiosely by its inhabitants as the twenty-first arrondissement of Paris.

These days, Dieppe, whose golf club's fairways stretch towards the Pourville road, has been forgotten. The great and the good have abandoned it and the big sea-front hotels no longer welcome great politicians, sportsmen and cultural personalities. Dieppe lost its reputation as a chic sea-side resort in the 1940's and has never regained its former glory. In an effort to recover it, however, the Dieppe golf club took advantage of its centenary celebrations to display its new logo, a three-masted vessel and two crossed irons with the dates 1897-1997. The Dieppe golf club has in fact made it into the select band of golf clubs which are over a hundred years old, of which there are only eight in mainland France.

Unlike on the more ancient course of Pau in the Atlantic Pyrenees, which has retained a sizeable part of last century's lay-out, today's lady golfers in their

As a mark of tribute to the 6th of June 1944, the third hole of La Mer, Omaha Beach, is called General de Gaulle.   ▽

Preceding pages:
The Etretat golf course is perched on top of the cliffs, at more than fifty metres above the sea.
◁◁

With the New Golf and the Amirauté, Saint-Gatien makes up the golfing trio of Deauville.
▽

Conviviality and good food are the lifeblood of the Saint-Gatien club.

bermuda shorts do not tread the same fairways as did their crinoline-skirted forbears in their broad-brimmed hats decorated with ribbons.

The first nine holes designed by the architect Willie Park ran along the cliff on the right of the road leading to the village of Pourville. With a more than eighty metre drop onto the strand below, the course was then the most spectacular in France.

The first French golfing magazine, Tennis et Golf, founded by Michael Daninos in 1914 describes, in its August 1922 edition, the spectacular game to be played there. "The Dieppe links crosses narrow gorges in the middle of fields of gorse and has stupendous views of the whole coast. Although picturesque, these holes are no walk-over. Nerves of steel and a sense of mountaineering are needed to make a successful drive from these steep hills. The void held the most insidious fascination for our golf balls and far too many of them vanished down onto the strand under the timorous eyes of their owners."

There are only a few yellowing postcards left to remind us of this fin de siècle golf course. The cliffs are being eroded at the rate of fifty centimetres per year and the holes are edging little by little towards the strand. This resulted in the Dieppe course, extended in 1912 by the great English architect Tom Simpson, the genius who created Chantilly, Chiberta and Fontainebleau, spreading onto the other side of the road onto a vast plateau from which, at the ninth hole, the church steeple of Varengeville rises.

The Etretat cliffs also have stories to tell. This seaside town nestles between high white cliffs. On its right is the monument to the aviators Nungesser and Coli; on the left, L'Aiguille Creuse, territory of the gentleman burglar, Arsène Lupin, creation of the Norman writer, Maurice Leblanc.

On these white cliffs, which the sea unceasingly gnaws away at with each tide to form natural arches, one drives at the same level as the seagulls are flying, one hundred metres above the waves. Although the course itself is only of average interest, its site makes it one of the most spectacular in Europe. The tenth hole, a double par five dogleg all uphill even attracts the attention of those out for their Sunday stroll. Their hands deep in their wind-cheaters, they are privy to the spectacle of golfers labouriously pulling their trolleys uphill or playing some big straight iron shots.

Like all links on the coast, Etretat is windy. On this empty plateau, scattered with a few scanty copses, the wind blows unremittingly and a wobbly swing easily comes acropper. On the putting greens, the pins are small and the flagsticks bend in the gusts. When the elements really unleash their power, the course gains in excitement and invention is the name of the game. The British, who come off the boats at Dieppe, are very good at this type of play. On the limestone cliffs of Sussex on the other side of the Channel, they experience these wind-swept playing conditions daily. They are the hallmark of seaside golf. The views are often breath-taking, the air is clean and bracing, but play can become rather an ordeal.

On the links of the Dunes de Granville course in the Manche department, the sea cannot be seen. But its scent is on the air, there is a strong smell of sea-spray, it can be heard and listened to. The Granville links, one of France's purest, is like a beach at low tide with its never-ending sun-scorched fairways, undulating terrain hinting at sandtraps and with as many circles of verdant lawn as of green. When the wind gets up, the delicate grasses of the roughs ripple and wave, playing with the light, and it looks like a beach at high tide.

The Manche department is the land of links and nine-hole courses. Apart from the twenty-seven holes at the Granville golf course and the recent extension to eighteen holes of the Agon-Coutainville course, the Cotentin courses are all nine holes. Gems for those who like fuss-free golf and Scottish-looking courses. Bréhal, south of Coutances, is an unpretentious and utterly charming nine hole course where every gust of wind means that the teeing grounds have to be cleared to stop them turning into bunkers. These courses are a far cry from the more sophisticated courses of nearby Calvados, a department whose number of eighteen-hole courses rivals that of the Riviera. Indeed, between Caen and Deauville there are seven eighteen-hole courses within forty kilometres. Four are less than four kilometres from

With its ubiquitous water hazards, the Amirauté club has retained vestiges of the marshes on which it was built.
◁

At the Amirauté, nine holes are lit at night, but only if requested beforehand.
◁

Deauville : the New Golf de Deauville, Saint-Julien, Saint-Gatien and L'Amirauté. A true resort in the Livarot and Calvados area, between the Auge country and the Côte Fleurie, where the golfers contest with the thoroughbreds for the rich meadows around the manor houses and castles.

At the New Golf de Deauville, the piece of wall standing at the teeing ground of the thirteenth hole bears witness to the

At the New Golf de Deauville, players putt under the windows of the Grand Hotel.
△

Only one piece of wall remains of the Marquis de Lassay's castle at the New Golf de Deauville.
▷

history of the Mont Canisy lands from which Deauville and, in the distance, Honfleur can be seen. "If you can't see Honfleur, it means that it's raining, and when you can see Honfleur, it means that it is about to rain," runs a local saying. This wall, ornamented with openwork and covered with weeds is the spectre of decadent nights in the Marquis de Lassay's castle in the eighteenth century. A line has now been drawn under those times in Deauville.

The official brochures state that this seaside resort did not come into its own until the nineteenth century with the Duc de Morny, half-brother of Napoleon III and grandson of Talleyrand. The development continued at the beginning of the twentieth century when Eugène Cornuché built the hotels Normandy and Royal and culminated with François André who, according to legend, traced out the plan for the Golf hotel in the snow with the tip of his umbrella. Its reception room windows opened out (and still do) onto the fairways designed by Tom Simpson. In the distance lies Deauville bay. The New Golf de Deauville retains the charm of its old course : it is not too long or too difficult and is planted with a large variety of trees, oak, elm, ash and the inevitable apple trees which are the symbol of the Auge country. On the Deauville beaches one passes the jet-set and the newly wealthy. At the golf club, some old members look back fondly to the lightning visits made by Bobby Jones, Jimmy Demaret or Robert de Vincenzo. At Cabourg, Marcel Proust's ghost haunts the grand hotel. The great French writer never soiled his gaiters on the Cabourg-le-Home course at Varaville. A pity, for an exhaustive description in one of the volumes of A la Recherche du Temps

Perdu would have improved our understanding of this dunes course with eleven par threes ! Today there are only six left. The most famous one, the Camembert, a round green atop a hillock, was devoured by mechanical diggers. So Cabourg-le-Home has become a more or less ordinary course. Its par three sixteenth does go some way to repair the damage with its dune-top green which seems to float in the westerly wind.

All throughout its history, Normandy has been a land of conquests and re-conquests. The most spectacular demonstration of these great deeds of battle are to be found in the museum of the Bayeux Tapestry. On more than one hundred metres of cloth, the tapestry, almost an embroidered cartoon strip, relates the epic of William the Conqueror, who crushed the English at the Battle of Hastings in 1066. A few kilometres from the capital of Bessin, open-air museums and military cemeteries recall the heroic landings of the Allied troops on the 6th June 1944. The golf course of Omaha Beach, code name of the beach which was to be the scene of the biggest military operation of all time, has honoured its liberators by giving each hole on the La Mer et du Bocage course the name of one of the heroes of the 6th of June. There are memorial plaques bearing the names of Eisenhower, De Gaulle, Leclerc, which were unveiled to the haunting strains of Bill Millin's bagpipes, Scottish infantryman and the first to cross, at dawn June 6th 1944, the Ouistreham iron bridge under German machine gun fire. From the green of the sixth hole of the La Mer course, a wonderful par four when the wind blows in from the sea, can be seen the remains of the artificial port of Arromanches, where hundreds of warships berthed during the month of June 1944.

The putting green surrounds a flower-covered well ; a must for anyone who wants to get to know Tom Simpson's subtle sloping greens.

A thousand years earlier, the golf course of the Champ de Bataille, at Neubourg in the Eure was the battleground for two great armies which fought for possession of the Duchy of Normandy. On this historic site, soaked with the blood of

At Omaha Beach, the drive seems to be suspended over the Port-en-Bessin fishing port.
△

From the sixth green of the La Mer's Omaha Beach course, the remains of the artificial port of Arromanches can be made out.
▷

Houlgate unfolds its undulating fairways in the Norman bocage landscape. △

The eighteenth hole of Houlgate appears to lead to the wonderful little castle of Beuzeval, now converted into flats.
▷

soldiers of a bygone age, the Champ de Bataille castle was built. A golf course was laid out on this estate, whose French-style gardens border forests of ancient trees. Its eighteen holes cross a valley of rhododendrons, leap waterfalls and pools, skirt a sand quarry and play with perfectly-ordered gardens which lead back to a clubhouse lodged in the former castle stables. In days of yore, after grand cavalcades through the Norman countryside, thoroughbreds came to rest here on the soft meadows, which have now become a golfers' and greenkeepers' paradise.

When the rhododendrons are in bloom, the Champ de Bataille course is adorned with thousands of colours.

Brittany

sible to find a suitable golf course." Choosing the site was a delicate matter and potential courses from Dinard to Saint-Lunaire were considered before the course finally ended up on the Saint-Briac dunes, more than seven kilometres from Dinard, just after the Garde-Guérin Point. The club, however, still carries the name of Dinard, much to the displeasure of Brice Lalonde, the Mayor of the municipality and ex-minister of the Fifth Republic.

The eighteen holes, which have been shifted, re-modelled and re-named since they were first laid out by Tom Dunn, follow the jagged cliffs of the eastern point of the Emerald coast. At the high points, two wooden benches donated by the club President and his son, compel you to take a beneficial break between swings, to enjoy views across the bay of Loncieux and its island chains. The vista is so beautiful that the golf club found itself having to fend off unscrupulous property developers. So the land as well as the clubhouse, a jewel of the 1920's, have been placed under protection. The golf club has been saved, but it nevertheless quite a headache for the stewards who have now to refer to the authorities for permission even to move a bunker.

Inside the one-storey clubhouse, the guard rail of the stairs which lead to the cloakrooms depicts interlaced golf clubs in wrought iron and the trophy cabinets could also be listed as part of the national golf heritage. For Dinard is to Brittany what Chantaco and La Nivelle are to the Basque country – a breeding ground for golf prodigies. As an expression of gratitude to the club that nursed them in their infancy, the now grown-up baby champions donate their trophies to it. The most prestigious, the Espirito Trophy, gleams in its cabinet. It was won at the World Team Amateur Championship and donated by Claudine Cros-Chartier, member of the 1964 French team with Catherine Lacoste, President of Chantaco. Other Dinard progeny have their names engraved into the dark wood of the club's honours board. Here we find Sven Boinet, winner of the Spanish International in 1975, Philippe Ploujoux, hero of the British Amateur in 1981, which gave him the honour of playing in the next two years in the two first rounds of the Masters in Augusta in the USA with the great Arnold Palmer.

The course designed by the French architect Alain Prat on the cliffs of the municipality of Pléneuf-le-Val-André in the Côtes d'Armor, is not yet of an age to reminisce and wallow in nostalgia ; it is too young and tradition will come later. For this sea resort only comes to life in the summer and for a long time, golf was limited to miniature golf matches on the lawns of the

Dinard's stair railing showing interlaced clubs in wrought iron. △

The Dinard links is over a century old and its holes are on the jagged cliffs of the Emerald coast.

◁

Following pages: Pléneuf-Val André's eighteen holes are a true masterpiece. The ninth hole and its green, which seems to become part of the sea, are the high point.
▷▷

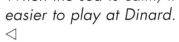
When the sea is calm, it is easier to play at Dinard.
◁

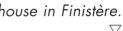
The Cornouaille course clubhouse in Finistère.
▽

municipal casino. These eighteen holes for children with their windmills, bridges and castles awakened many a golfing ambition, indeed that of the author himself, but sadly it has now been covered with tarmac to provide a car park - a pity !

When the new Val André course, this time a proper eighteen holes, replaced the temporary structures with a permanent clubhouse, the builders were careful to place the bay windows of the dining room towards Vedelet, a small island, rising up out of the sea like a pyramid, behind the port of

Pléneuf-Val André's eleventh hole is one of the most best par fives in France : it must be played off the back tees.△

The early morning mist spreads its white mantle over Pléneuf-Val André's fairways. ◁

Piégu. A bird sanctuary, the island can only be visited for a few hours during the spring tides when the sea recedes sufficiently to uncover a path.

In front of the restaurant is the backtee of the tenth hole, a par four which begins the short sea sequence. For the drive, you have to aim at the Nantua beach straight ahead to reach the blind fairway leading to a green below. This hole is reminiscent of the eleventh hole of the Sperone course in Corsica. The next is the signature hole of Pléneuf-le-Val-André which is familiar throughout Europe from the pages of glossy magazines and dreamt of by golfers all over the world. In order to make the most of the outline of this par five, you have to climb to the top of the tiny rocky platform which acts as a teeing ground for the very good players. Whether the balls are yellow, white or black, it no longer matters. What harm if one loses a ball or indeed two ! It matters little, for the spectacle is more important than a golf ball. On the left, fifty metres below, the Vallées beach extends into the huge Nantua beach. On the right of this long strip of immaculate sand, the fairway leads to an irregularly-shaped putting green. A small ruined house, with the windows wide open and two twisted pine trees at the left of the fairway entrance are the landmarks for establishing position, as buoys and beacons are for the sailor. To reach the lawn, the ball has to travel nearly one hundred and eighty metres. This is not for the faint-hearted ! Those who cannot face this dizzyingly spectacular teeing ground may take a break for

Following pages:
La Bretèche golf course winds around the moats of this fourteenth century castle.
▷▷

- 167 -

Ploemeur-Océan is Morbihan's, indeed Brittany's, most beautiful links.▷

The outbuildings of La Bretèche castle have been made into a club-house and a hotel.
▽

a few minutes on the green of this par five to admire this hole in reverse, from the green to the teeing ground. At sunset it is an unforgettable sight !

In the south in Morbihan there are standing stones and dolmens, cairns and burial mounds which date from four thousand years B.C. Hewn from granite, these giant stones, some standing, some fallen or some piled up, describe formations or circles which even today give rise to much debate. All sorts of hypotheses have been put forward, but no one scientific truth has been agreed upon. The region's every inhabitant has his own explanation, such as one Morbihan golf club steward who explains that all the standing stones form gigantic circles whose centre is the big standing stone and La Table des Marchands de Locmariaquer. These moorland stones, dear to Obelix, are today under threat and are being carefully looked after. At Carnac, a Mecca for these megaliths, the formations are surrounded by wire fencing so that nature can re-establish itself and allow these ancient stones weighing hundreds of kilos to re-embed themselves in their surroundings.

Like the standing stones of Carnac, the Morbihan golf courses form a circle from Ploemeur Océan to Lorient and Sauzon sur Belle Ile. In the centre lies the Saint-Laurent course, a few kilometres from Carnac.

This course does not, however, conceal megalithic treasures, standing stones or dolmens. In the United States the promoters would have seized on this symbolism, but not in France. Perhaps because Saint-Laurent could be mistaken for a Landes region course, with its pines, pines and more pines. The fairways are quite flat on the way out and undulating on the way back. The greens are narrow and bunkers never punish a shot that it is too short. It is a clear example of an English course (the architect is Michael Fenn). To find the Brittany of the far-travelling seafarers one has to go to Belle Ile. On the clifftop of its western point, the ninth, tenth and thirteenth holes of Sauzon - depending on the year - invite meditation upon the power of the elements. Sauzon has already lost several holes thanks to its notorious storms, and the salt-laden spray seems set to put an eventual stop to man's best efforts. In the interim, however, until the golf course is actually lying at the foot of the cliffs or has been left fallow, the dare must be taken up of challenging the second hole's putting green which lies in the sea, defended like a fortress, accessible only with the help of sea breezes.

It would be difficult to bring this journey round Brittany to a close without mentioning the "frontier" courses of La Bretèche and La Baule. For Missillac,

Short of space on their old site, the La Baule members chose to move eight kilometres inland.

The President of the Dinard club and his son have put some benches next to the green so that the players can enjoy the landscape.
△

Water hazards are the golfer's companion at La Baule. Here one is in the heart of La Brière.
▽

△ Two years after opening, La Baule and its clubhouse, with its charming roof, hosted the French Open in 1978.

on the Vannes road, is only a few kilometres from Morbihan, a few par fives away from Brittany, the place dear to the heart of the inhabitants of this little village on the Nantes-Vannes main road, which used to be defended by the crenellated towers of La Bretesche castle. These days this moat-surrounded castle no longer inspires fear. Now converted into flats it discreetly guards the two hundred hectare estate and the eighteen holes of the fairways lying beneath its crenels. One of the tenants, Gérard Métairie has a look at his beloved golf course every morning. About twenty years ago, this property developer, egged on by his friends, decided to build a golf course. When looking for someone to build the course, the name of the great English champion of the 1930's and 1940's, and triple winner of the British Open, Henry Cotton was suggested. He came to Missillac, made some sketches and sent in his estimate. "Too expensive," retorted the promoter and called on another Englishman, Bill Baker. Like Métairie he enjoys hunting and this shared passion drew them together. The project was fine-tuned between hunting shots and Bill Baker secured the commission. With its resolutely British cottages and the hotel converted from the outbuildings and stables, the Bretesche golf club appeals to golf-trotters who like old stonemasonry. For although the castle, the access to which is

The owner of the vast Ormes estate, Yvonnic de la Chesnais, has made it into an eighteen hole course and ... a camping ground.

At Brest-Iroise, the rocks along the fairways and the greens are part of the course : the balls cannot resist them.
△

Landes scenery with broom trees and woods at Brest-Iroise. The landscape is always full of interest.
▷

protected by a drawbridge, was renovated in the nineteenth century by Eugène Viollet-le-Duc, it looks as though it is straight out of a cloak and dagger film in which golf clubs should be replaced by long swords and visored caps by wide, plumed hats.

At La Baule the club members were urged to take a leap into the future when they started to feel cramped on the old course laid out by François André, a driving force of the wild years. This smart seaside resort to the north-east of Nantes, whose eight kilometre

Baden golf course in Morbihan looks over the estuary of the Auray river where sailors enjoy themselves. △

beach is unique in France, wanted a golf course that would match its reputation. With the Lucien Barrière group at the helm, owners of the New Golf de Deauville, this new course would play both the tourism and the prestige card. Two years after opening, La Baule hosted the French Open in 1978. This was a wonderful opportunity to promote this truly French-style resort and to publicise the twenty-seven holes designed by Dave Thomas and Peter Alliss and re-modelled by Michel Gayon. Not to mention the hotel, whose windows look out onto a five hectare lake, a nod to La Brière,

At Belle Ile the number of holes varies from year to year; whether it is twelve or thirteen depends upon the whim of the spring tides. ▽

the marshy region extending from Saint-Nazaire to Missillac. La Baule is only thirty kilometres from Morbihan but the traditions of Breton history pay little heed to borders drawn with a scalpel in Parisian offices.

Poto: J.M.Collas. OTSI Belle Ile en Mer

*I*n the Bordeaux Region

A Fragrant Bouquet

In the Bordeaux Region

Although not classified as premiers crus 1855, for golf had not then reached France, the Bordeaux courses have a heady aroma. Like the region's great vintages, they improve with age. And the new appellations such as Pian-Médoc and Seignosse are poised to become golf's Petrus.

This par three of the Châteaux course is more intimidating than difficult. Everything depends on where the pin is placed. △

The two eighteen-hole courses of the Médoc, designed by Bill Coore and Rod Whitman, are both American-style and authentic links. ◁

*Preceding pages:
Château Latour, surrounded by its vineyard, produces one of the best Bordeaux vintages.* ◁◁

Bordeaux is the world capital of wine. From the world over, expert oenologists come here to taste its heavenly nectar. The hundred thousand hectares of Bordeaux's vineyards produce five hundred million bottles of wine a year for the fine palates of the world market. Médoc, Saint-Emilion, Côtes, Graves, Saint-Julien ... whites, reds and rosés excite the appetites of those who love fine wine. For Bordeaux wines are the world's best. 1855 was the year in which the wine merchants' brokers established a system of classification for the great vintages, which more than a century and a half later remains undisputed. Only one wine, the Mouton-Rothschild, successfully passed the entrance test in 1973 allowing it to be included on this prestigious list of the world's best vintages. Château-Lafite, Château-Margaux, Château-Latour, Château Haut-Brion ... in Bordeaux, wine is intertwined with these family residences overlooking the vineyards. Stone and vine are the Bordeaux symbols of wealth.

At the new golf club of Pian-Médoc, magnums, jeroboams or mathusalems of the great classified vintages decorate the clubhouse bar and the restaurant cellar is one of the best supplied with grands crus and can easily compete with the Augusta National's in the USA, which hosts the Masters every April. From the outset, Pian-Médoc counted on the region's treasury of wines to forge a reputation that would go beyond its borders. On the Les Châteaux course each teeing ground is named after a Médoc vintage and during the last French Open huge bottles (plastic of course) on the practice greens were used as landmarks and for judging distance by the professionals.

The course of Les Châteaux is a true inland links designed by the American architect Bill Coore and the American champion Ben Crenshaw. The broom

Behind this green on the Châteaux course is the clubhouse with its exceptional wine cellar. The 135 is not a new Bordeaux vintage, but a landmark (wink, wink !) for the practice green during the French Open.

trees along its fairways are reminiscent of the links along the Irish and Scottish coasts. The American architect, who started out with Pete Dye, has exploited the winds coming in off the Atlantic to design a strategy-demanding eighteen holes with greens that have to be judged carefully. The other eighteen holes, Les Vignes, designed by the Canadian Rod Whitman, lie in the benevolent shadow of a pine forest. By virtue of hosting two of the European circuit's doubles tournaments and the French Open in 1999, hundreds of professional players have become ambassadors of the Médoc abroad. And Angel Cabrera, winner of the driving contest at the last French Open, returned to Argentina weighed down with eighty bottles of the great Bordeaux vintages. A good piece of publicity in Buenos Aires for these exceptional vineyards.

With the foundation in the 1980's and 1990's of the Pian-Médoc, Caudéran, Gujan-Mestras Lacanau, Graves et Sauternais (well-named) and Bordeaux-Lac (on the initiative of the mayor, a player of golf and tennis, Jacques Chaban-Delmas), golf has left the confined spaces of the Golf Bordelais, club of the Bordeaux upper classes. Built on a former clay

This land was drained in the reign of Napoleon III. A century later, Alain Prat recreated seven ponds on the Gujan Mestras course.

Lacanau, famous for its surf, has forged itself a reputation as a golfing venue with its pine-shaded fairways.

pigeon shoot, the Golf Bordelais course still retains the air of an old-fashioned course. The short holes and the shallow greens lie in a wooded park. With four thousand seven hundred metres for a par sixty seven the Golf Bordelais no longer seems to live up to the idea of a modern golf course. For today's players want distance, distance and more distance to be able to give the ball a slam with their titanium woods; provided, of course, that the fairways are wide enough for them to be liberally "sprinkled" with big hooks and slices. These "new age" golfers find the Golf Bordelais rather frustrating, because playing here demands more subtlety than strength and more accuracy of aim than distance.

To satisfy their desire for a power game, golfers take the coast road at the weekend to the Arcachon basin where all of Bordeaux disperses between the resorts of Arcachon and Cap Ferret and the golf clubs of Gujan-Mestras

and Arcachon. The first, designed by the Frenchman François Alain Prat is American-style with seven ponds for target golf; the second is an English-style course at the foot of the Pylat dune which rises to one hundred and fifteen metres above the ocean.

Although these courses are only a few kilometres apart, almost one hundred years separates them in age. The first holes of the Arcachon course, now long gone, were laid in 1895 by an Anglican Church pastor, Samuel Radcliff. After the Second World War, the biggest Arcachon families clubbed together to re-create the course and invited the great Basque Pierre Hirigoyen to sniff out the ideal site which he finally found in the Teste-sur-Buch municipality. Hole by hole, year by year the golf course gradually took shape and the founding members had to make full use of their imagination to have matches worthy of the name on only three holes, then five, then nine before closing the loop with a proper eighteen-hole course on which one did not have go back to the beginning every half an hour.

This caution is now ancient history. Courses are now built in one go and the golf course opens as soon as the initial design is finished, as long as the course can satisfy the authorities as to the administrative problems that crop up without fail when a course abuts onto the shoreline. At Moliets, for

Moliets is not only famous for its wide fairways under the pines but also for its five seaside holes.
◁

The iron game must be of the utmost precision on the rambling fair-ways of the magnifi-cent Seignosse course.
▽

example, Robert Trent Jones had to work to a very tight set of specifications in order to preserve the ocean-facing pines – a fortunate move which gives this eighteen-hole course of six thousand one hundred and seventy two metres a look of the Landes with its wide fairways carved out of the pine forest and its tucs, small hilly dunes, which the architect has exploited to great advantage. With its four holes along the sea-shore, from the thirteenth to the sixteenth, Moliets, with Saint-Jean-de-Monts in the Vendée and Chiberta in the Eastern Pyrenees, is one of the three true Atlantic links.

As the road descends towards the Basque region, it becomes a hundred kilometre long straight line which cuts through the pine forests of the Landes. This long monotonous strip of asphalt leads to Biarritz and Spain. Just before reaching the Basque country golf enthusiasts turn off the main road and go towards the village of Capbreton to reach Seignosse, Blue Green Chain's most beautiful acquisition. It is a veritable monument to golfing glory. Wonderful, winding, magnificent, sadistic even, this jewel buried in the forests of the Landes can only be described in extremes, proof that it is a great course, for would a mediocre course give rise to such passions ? An expert in these matters, José-Maria Olazabal comes from Fontarrabie in

The situation is clear from the outset at Seignosse : narrow fairways, greens surrounded by water. Although the spectacle is worth going out of one's way for, the scorecard is rarely flattering.
◁/△

The pigeon loft near Vigiers'
last green.
▷

Between swings, the golfer
can savour the luscious plums
that the owner of the property uses to make jam.
▽

Spain to train here, when his tournament schedule allows. Twice victorious at the Masters, he can work on his iron game here, which is said to be one of the best in the world. At Seignosse absolute precision is necessary to achieve a good score, for the American architect Robert Van Hagge has excessively complicated this course of doglegs, green approaches and slopes. With their fragile swing sorely tested, average players are quick to criticise the course design. Once they have accepted their poor showing, however, they swiftly change tack and praise the beauty of this undulating course in the middle of the forest, where the sun's rays filter through the trees, and promise themselves that they will return once more to subdue the monster.

When the golfers of Bordeaux have had their fill of sea, sand and pine forests, they like to wander into the vineyards, which stretch for dozens of kilometres on both sides of the Garonne, and cross Sauternes to dream in

△
President François Mitterrand used to enjoy a round with his friends on the Hossegor course in the Landes.
▷

Preceding pages:
The last iron shot towards the eighteenth green. Behind it is the castle of Vigiers, nicknamed "Little Versailles".
◁◁

front of Château Yqeum, the vineyard which produces the most sumptuous and syrupy white wine in the world. It is a nectar fit for the Gods; a hundred page paean to it can be found in wondrous language in the philosopher, Michel Serres' book, The Five Senses. Château Yquem reveals all the subtelty of its bouquet, when savoured with foie gras du Périgord, such as that prepared by the chef at Les Fresques, the gourmet restaurant of Vigiers castle in Monestier in the Dordogne. The restaurant terrace looks out onto the golf course designed by British architect Donald Steel, in the middle of the countryside a hundred kilometres from Bordeaux. Lars Petersson, the owner, was the first to fall in love with this castle, called "the little Versailles" in the seventeenth century, although it bears no resemblance to the palace of the Sun King. To rekindle the fortunes of this small castle at La Mansart, this Swede, a former shipowner, invested almost one hundred million francs for the comfort of his guests, foreigners for the most part, who come to spend their leisure-time golfing on the eighteen holes bordered by plum trees or fishing for barbel in the course's lake. At Vigiers, the golfers live the life of the castle, and at evening, by candlelight, it is of course, the finest wines that gleam in the Bordeaux glasses !

Bibliography

"Golf-Club de Mandelieu: histoire d'un centenaire, 1891-19910" by Bernard Vadon, B.C. edition.

"Le golf de La Nivelle" by Gérard Dunoyer, Guy Lalanne and Frédéric Paillard, Association sportive de La Nivelle.

"Cent ans de golf à Dieppe" by Olivier Merlin, Editions Bertout editions.

"La France des golfs, guide 1999-2000", Golf Magazine-Emap France

"Peugeot Golf Guide", 1998 edition, D. & G. Motte editions

"The Architects of Golf" by Geoffrey S. Cornish and Ronald E. Whitten, Harper Collins editions.

"Pau Golf Club, le St Andrews du continent", by Yves Caillé, J & D editions.

Magazines "Tennis et Golf", 1914-1970 collections.

Magazines "Golf Européen", 1970-1999 collections.

Glossary

Birdie : one shot below par

Bogey : one shot above par

Bunker : hollowed-out sand-filled obstacle
There are fairway bunkers and green bunkers
Some may have patches of lawn

Dogleg : a hole curving to the right or to the left

Eagle : two shots below par

Fairway : the part of the hole consisting of mown grass between the tee and the green

Green : the closely-mown part of the course where the hole is indicated by a flagstick

Greenkeeper : person responsible for maintaining the course

Hook : when the ball flies markedly to the left or to the right

Inland : an inland course

Links : course between the sea and the sand-dunes

Par : the ideal score for a particular hole
One course may have 3's, 4's and 5's

Rough : the unmown part of the course bordering the fairways and the greens

Slice : same as hook

Tee : starting point of a hole

The Best French Golf Courses

A "Tour de France" of the one hundred and fifty best French courses in alphabetical order. The name of the department is in brackets after the town in which they are situated.

La Rochelle has the appearance of a links.
△

Following the example of the Scots, the French enjoy their passion for golf in the morning mist.
◁

F = 100 to 200 French Francs
FF = 200 to 300 French Francs
FFF = above 300 French Francs
Price for weekends and bank holidays in high season
H: Hotel on the golf course

Ammerschwihr
Route des Trois Epis
Ammerschwihr (Haut-Rhin)
Tel.: 03 89 47 17 30
Architect: Robert Berthet
FF

Apremont - 18 holes
CD 606
Apremont (Oise)
Tel.: 03 44 25 61 11
Architect: John Jacobs
FFF

Arcachon - 18 holes
35, boulevard d'Arcachon
La Teste-sur-Buch (Gironde)
Tel.: 05 56 54 44 00
Architectes: Cecil Blandford et Pierre Hirigoyen
FF

Arcangues - 18 holes
Arcangues (Pyrénées-Atlantiques)
Tel.: 05 59 43 10 56
Architect: Ronald Fream
FFF

Ariège - 18 holes
Unjat
La Bastide-de-Serou (Ariège)
Té.: 05 61 64 56 78
Architect: Michel Gayon
F

Avrillé - 18 holes
Avrillé (Maine-et-Loire)
Tel.: 02 41 69 22 50
Architect: Robert Berthet
FF

Baden - 18 holes
Kernic
Baden (Morbihan)
Tel.: 02 97 57 18 96
Architect: Yves Bureau
FF

Barbaroux - 18 holes - H
Route de Cabasse
Brignoles (Var)
Tel.: 04 94 69 63 63
Architect: P. B. Dye
FFF

Beauvallon - 18 holes
Boulevard des Collines
Maxime (Var)
Tel.: 04 94 96 16 98
FFF

Bélesbat - 18 holes
Domaine de Bélesbat - 18 holes - H
Boutigny-sur-Essonne (Essonne)
Tel.: 01 69 23 19 10
Architectes: Marc Adam et Patrick Fromanger
FFF

Belle Dune - 18 holes
Fort-Mahon Plage (Somme)
Tel.: 03 22 23 45 50
Architect: Jean-Manuel Rossi
FF

Belle-Ile - 13 holes
Sauzon
Le Palais (Morbihan)
Tel.: 02 97 31 64 65
F

Béthemont - 18 holes
12, rue du Parc de Béthemont
Poissy (Yvelines)
Tel.: 01 39 75 51 13
Architect: Bernhard Langer
FFF

Besançon - 18 holes
La Chevillotte
Mamirolle (Doubs)
Tel.: 03 81 55 73 54
Architect: Michael Fenn
FF

Biarritz-le-Phare - 18 holes
2, avenue Edith Cavell
Biarritz (Pyrénées-Atlantiques)
Tel.: 05 59 03 71 80
Architect: Willie Dunn
FFF

Bigorre - 18 holes
Pouzac
Bagnères-de-Bigorre (Hautes-Pyrénées)
Tel.: 05 62 91 06 20
Architect: Olivier Brizon
F

Bitche - 27 holes
Rue des Prés
Bitche (Meurthe-et-Moselle)
Tel.: 03 87 96 15 30
Architect: Marc Adam et Patrick Fromanger
FF

Bondues - 36 holes
Château de la Vigne
Bondues (Nord)
Tel.: 03 20 23 20 62
Architectes: Fred Hawtree et
Robert Trent Jones
FFF

Bordeaux-Lac - 36 holes
Avenue de Pernon
Bordeaux (Gironde)
Tel.: 05 56 50 92 72
FF

Bordelais - 18 holes
Rue de Kater
Bordeaux-Caudéran (Gironde)
Tel.: 05 56 28 56 04
FF

Bossey - 18 holes
Château de Crevin
Bossey (Haute-Savoie)
Tel.: 04 50 43 95 50
Architect: R.Trent Jones Jr
FFF

Bresse - 18 holes
Domaine de Mary
Condeissiat (Ain)
Tel.: 04 74 51 42 09
Architect: Jérémy Pern
FF

Brest-Iroise - 27 holes - H
Parc de Lann Rohou
Landerneau (Finistère)
Tel.: 02 98 85 16 17
Architect: Michael Fenn
FF

Cabourg-le Home - 18 holes
Avenue du Président Coty
Le Home-Varaville (Calvados)
Tel.: 02 31 91 25 56
Architectes: Jackon et Olivier
Brizon
FF

Cannes-Mandelieu - 18 holes
Route du Golf
Mandelieu (Alpes-Maritimes)
Tel.: 04 93 49 55 39
Architect: Harry S. Colt
FFF

Cannes-Mougins - 18 holes
175, avenue du Golf

Mougins (Alpes-Maritimes)
Tel.: 04 93 75 79 13
Architect: Peter Alliss et David
Thomas
FFF

Carcassonne - 18 holes - H
Route de Saint-Hilaire
Carcassonne (Aude)
Tel.: 06 13 20 85 43
Architect: Jean-Pierre Basurco
FF

Cély-en-Bière - 18 holes
Route de Saint-Germain
Cély-en-Bière (Seine-et-Marne)
Tel.: 01 64 38 03 07
Architect: Marc Adam et
Patrick Fromanger
FFF

Chamonix - 18 holes - H
35, route du Golf, les Praz
Chamonix (Haute-Savoie)
Tel.: 04 50 53 06 28
Architect: Robert Trent Jones
Sr
FFF

Champ de Bataille - 18 holes
Le Neubourg (Eure)
Tel.: 02 32 35 03 72
Architectes: Robin Nelson et
Thierry Huau
FFF

Chantaco - 18 holes
Route d'Ascain
Saint-Jean-de-Luz (Pyrénées-
Atlantiques)
Tel.: 05 59 26 14 22
Architect: Harry S. Colt
FFF

Chantilly - 36 holes
Allée de la Ménagerie
Chantilly (Oise)
Tel.: 03 44 57 04 43
Architect: Tom Simpson
FFF (en semaine uniquement)

Château de Chailly - 18
holes - H
Chailly-sur-Armançon (Côte
d'Or)
Tel.: 03 80 90 30 40
Architectes: Thierry Sprecher

et Gery Watine
FFF

Château de Cheverny - 18
holes
La Rousselière
Cheverny (Loir-et-Cher)
Tel.: 02 54 79 24 70
Architect: Olivier Van der
Vynck
FF

Château des Ormes - 18
holes - H
Epiniac
Dol-de-Bretagne (Ille-et-Vilaine)
Tel.: 02 99 73 54 44
Architect: Antoine
d'Ormesson
FF

Château de Raray - 27 holes
- H
4, rue Nicolas de Lancy
Raray (Oise)
Tel.: 03 44 54 70 61
Architect: Patrice Léglise
FFF

Château des Sept Tours - 18
holes - H
Courcelles-de-Touraine (Indre-
et-Loire)
Tel.: 02 47 24 69 75
Architectes: Donald
Harradine et Olivier Dongradi
FF

Château des Vigiers - 18
holes - H
Monestier (Dordogne)

*It is thanks to a local farmer that
the fairways of the marvellous La
Bigorre course can stretch to the
foot of the Pyrenees*

Tel.: 05 53 61 50 33
Architect: Donald Steel
FFF

Chiberta - 18 holes - H
104, boulevard des Plages
Anglet (Pyrénées-Atlantiques)
Tel.: 05 59 52 51 10
Architect: Tom Simpson
FFF

Clécy - 18 holes
Manoir de Cantelou
Clécy (Calvados)
Tel.: 02 31 69 72 72
Architect: Bill Baker
FF

Clément Ader - 18 holes
Gretz-Armainvilliers
Tel.: 01 64 07 34 10
Architectes: Michel Gayon et
Saito
FFF

Compiègne - 18 holes
Avenue Royale
Compiègne (Oise)
Tel.: 03 44 38 48 00
Architect: Freemantle
FF

Cornouaille - 18 holes
Manoir du Mesmeur
La Forêt-Fouesnant (Finistère)
Tel.: 02 98 56 97 09

Architect: Fred Hawtree
FF

Courson-Monteloup - 27 holes
Ferme de la Gloriette
Couson-Monteloup (Essonne)
Tel.: 01 64 58 80 80
Architect: Robert Von Hagge
FFF

Deauville l'Amirauté - 25 holes
CD 278
Tourgeville (Calvados)
Tel.: 02 31 14 42 00
Architect: Bill Baker
FFF

Dieppe - 18 holes
51, route de Pourville
Dieppe (Seine-Maritime)
Tel.: 02 35 84 25 05
Architect: Willie Park
FF

Dijon-Bourgogne - 18 holes
Bois de Norges
Norges-la-Ville (Côte d'Or)
Tel.: 03 80 35 71 10
Architect: Michael Fenn
FF

Dinard - 18 holes
Boulevard de la Houle
Saint-Briac-sur-Mer (Ille-et-Vilaine)
Tel.: 02 99 88 32 07

Architect: Tom Dunn
FFF
Disneyland Paris - 27 holes - H
Magny-le-Hongre (Seine-et-Marne)
Tel.: 01 60 45 68 90
Architect: Ronald Fream
FF

Divonne - 18 holes - H
Divonne-les-Bains (Ain)
Tel.: 04 50 40 34 11
Architect: M. Nakowsky et Donald Harradine
FFF

Esery - 27 holes
Esery (Haute-Savoie)
Tel.: 04 50 36 58 70
Architect: Michel Gayon
FFF

Etiolles - 27 holes
Vieux chemin de Paris
Etiolles (Essonne)
Tel.: 01 60 75 49 49
Architect: Michel Gayon
FFF

Etretat - 18 holes
Route du Havre
Etretat (Seine-Maritime)
Tel.: 02 35 27 04 89
Architectes: M. Chantepie et Didier Fruchet
FFF

Evian - 18 holes - H
Domaine du Royal Club Evian
Evian (Haute-Savoie)
Tel.: 04 50 75 46 66
Architect: Cabell Robinson

FFF

Falgos - 18 holes - H
Saint-Laurent-de-Cerdans (Pyrénées-Orientales)
Tel.: 04 68 39 51 42
FF

Feucherolles - 18 holes
Sainte-Gemme
Feucherolles (Yvelines)
Tel.: 01 30 54 94 94
Architect: Jean-Marie Poellot
FFF

Flaine-les-Carroz - 18 holes
Col de Pierre Carré
Flaine (Haute-Savoie)
Tel.: 04 50 90 85 44
Architect: Robert Berthet
FF

Fontainebleau - 18 holes
Route d'Orléans
Fontainebleau (Seine-et-Marne)
Tel.: 01 64 22 22 95
Architect: Tom Simpson
FFF

Fontcaude - 18 holes - H
Route de Lodève
Juvignac (Hérault)
Tel.: 04 67 03 34 30
Architect: Chris Pittman
FF

Fontenailles - 18 holes - H
Domaine du Bois Boudran
Fontenailles (Seine-et-Marne)
Tel.: 01 64 60 51 52
Architect: Michel Gayon
FFF

Forêt de Montpensier - 18 holes
Domaine du Château de Rihat
Serbannes (Allier)
Tel.: 04 70 56 58 39
FF

Frégate - 27 holes - H
Route de Bandol
Saint-Cyr-sur-Mer (Var)
tel.: 04 94 32 50 50

Architect: Ronald Fream
FFF

Gouverneur - 36 holes - H
Château du Breuil
Monthieux (Ain)
Tel.: 04 72 26 40 34
Architectes: Didier Fruchet, Georges Wil et Thierry Sprecher
FF

Grande-Bastide - 18 holes
Châteauneuf-de-Grasse (Alpes-Maritimes)
Tel.: 04 93 77 70 08
Architect: Cabell Robinson
FFF

Granville - 27 holes
Pavillon du Golf
Bréville-sur-Mer (Manche)
Tel.: 02 33 50 23 06
Architect: Harry S. Colt et Alison et Hawtree
FF

Grenoble-Bresson - 18 holes
Route de Montavie
Bresson (Isère)
Tel.: 04 76 73 65 00
Architect: R.Trent Jones Jr
FF

Gujan - 18 holes
Route de Sauguinet
Gujan-Mestras (Gironde)
Tel.: 05 57 52 73 73
Architect: Alain Prat
FF

Hardelot Les Dunes - 18 holes
Avenue Edouard VII
Hardelot (Pas-de-Calais)
Tel.: 03 21 91 90 90
Architect: Paul Rolin
FFF

Hardelot Les Pins - 18 holes
3, avenue du Golf
Hardelot (Pas-de-Calais)
Tel.: 03 21 83 73 10
Architect: Tom Simpson
FFF

Hossegor - 18 holes
Avenue du Golf
Hossegor (Landes)
Tel.: 05 58 43 56 99

Chailly castle in Burgundy offers one the chance to travel back in time to live castle life for a weekend.

Architect: John Morrison
FFF
Houlgate - 18 holes
Gonneville-sur-Mer (Calvados)
Tel.: 02 31 24 80 49
Architect: Dave Thomas
F

Ilbarritz - 9 holes
Avenue du Château
Bidart (Pyrénées-Atlantiques)
Tel.: 05 59 43 81 30
Architect: Pierre Thévenin
F

International Club du Lys - 36 holes
Rond-Point du Grand Cerf
Lamorlaye (Oise)
Tel.: 03 44 21 26 00
Architectes: Tom Simpson (Chênes), Robert Berthet (Bouleaux)
FFF

Joyenval - 36 holes
Chemin de la Tuilerie
Chambourcy (Yvelines)
Tel.: 01 39 22 27 50
Architect: R.Trent Jones Sr
FFF

Kempferhof - 18 holes - H
351, rue du Moulin
Plobsheim (Bas-Rhin)
Tel.: 03 88 98 72 72
Architect: Robert Von Hagge
FFF

La Baule - 27 holes
Saint-André-des-Eaux (Loire-Atlantiques)
Tel.: 02 40 60 46 18
Architectes: Peter Allis, Dave Thomas et Michel Gayon
FFF

La Boulie - 36 holes
Rue de Pont Colbert
Versailles (Yvelines)
Tel.: 01 39 50 59 41
Architect:
FFF

La Bretesche - 18 holes - H
Domaine de la Bretesche
Missillac (Loire-Atlantiques)
Tel.: 02 51 76 86 86

Architect: Bill Baker
FF
La Grande Motte - 42 holes - H
Avenue du Golf
La Grande Motte (Hérault)
Tel.: 04 67 56 05 00
Architect: Robert Trent Jones Sr
FF

La Nivelle - 18 holes
Place Sharp
Ciboure (Pyrénées-Atlantiques)
Tel.: 05 59 47 18 99
Architect: John Henry Taylor
FFF

La Largue - 18 holes
Rue du Golf
Mooslargue (Haut-Rhin)
Tel.: 03 89 07 67 67
Architect: Jean Garaialde
FFF

La Vaucouleurs - 36 holes
Rue de l'Eglise
Civry-la-Forêt (Yvelines)
Tel.: 01 34 87 62 29
Architect: Michel Gayon
FFF

Lac d'Annecy - 18 holes
Echarvines
Talloires (Haute-Savoie)
tel.: 04 50 60 12 89
Architect: Cecil Blandford
FF

Le Prieuré - 36 holes
Sailly (Yvelines)
Tel.: 01 34 76 65 65
Architect: Fred Hawtree
FFF

Le Sart - 18 holes
5, rue Jean Jaurès
Villeneuve d'Ascq (Nord)
Tel.: 03 20 72 02 51
Architect: Allan McBeth
FFF

Le Touquet - 45 holes - H
Avenue du Golf
Le Touquet (Pas-de-Calais)
Tel.: 03 21 06 28 00
Architect: Horace Hutchinson (la Forêt), Harry S. Colt (la

Mer)
FFF
Les Aisses - 27 holes
RN 20 sud
La Ferté-Saint-Aubin (Loiret)
Tel.: 02 38 64 80 87
Architect: Olivier Brizon
FF

Les Bordes - 18 holes - H
Saint-Laurent-Nouan (Loir-et-Cher)
Tel.: 02 54 87 72 13
Architect: Robert Von Hagge
FFF

L'Isle Adam - 18 holes
1, chemin des Vanneaux
L'Isle Adam (Val d'Oise)
Tel.: 01 34 08 11 11
Architect: Ronald Fream
FFF

Lons-le-Saunier - 18 holes - H
Vernantois (Jura)
Tel.: 03 84 43 04 80
Architect: Hugues Lambert
FF

Lyon - 36 holes
Villette d'Anthon (Isère)
Tel.: 04 78 31 11 13
Architect: Hugues Lambert
FF

Mâcon-La Salle - 18 holes
Mâcon nord
La Salle (Saône-et-Loire)
Tel.: 03 85 36 09 71

Pont Royal is the only French course designed by Severiano Ballasteros, the Spanish winner of five Major titles.
Architect: Robert Berthet
FF

Makila - 18 holes
Route de Cambo
Bassussary (Pyrénées-Atlantiques)
Tel.: 05 59 58 42 42
Architect: Rocky Roquemore
FFF

Médoc - 36 holes
Le Pian-Médoc (Gironde)
Tel.: 05 56 70 11 90
Architectes: Bill Coore (les Châteaux), Rod Whitman (Les Vignes)
FFF

Méribel - 18 holes
Méribel (Savoie)
Tel.: 04 79 00 52 67
Architectes: Gery Watine, Thierry Sprecher et Michael Fenn
FF

Mignaloux - 18 holes - H
635, route de Beauvoir
Mignaloux (Vienne)
Tel.: 05 49 46 70 27
Architect: Olivier Brizon
FF

Moliets - 27 holes - H
Rue Mathieu Desbieys
Moliets (Landes)
Tel.: 05 58 48 54 65

Architect: .Trent Jones Sr
FFF
Mont d'Arbois - 18 holes
Route du Mont d'Arbois
Mégève (Haute-Savoie)
Tel.: 04 50 21 29 79
Architect: Henry Cotton
FF

Montpellier-Massane - 18 holes - H
Domaine de Massane
Baillargues (Hérault)
Tel.: 04 67 87 87 87
Architect: Ronald Fream
FF

Monte-Carlo - 18 holes
Route du Mont Agel
La Turbie (Alpes-Maritimes)
Tel.: 04 93 41 09 11
FFF

Morfontaine - 27 holes
Mortefontaine (Oise)
Tel.: 03 44 54 68 27
Architect: Tom Simpson
Sur invitation d'un membre

National - 45 holes - H
2, avenue du Golf
Guyancourt (Yvelines)
Tel.: 01 30 43 36 00
Architectes (Albatros): Robert
Von Hagge, Hubert

The little known Sablé-sur-Sarthes course is unanimously recognised as a great course by the professional players of the Challenge Tour who play a tournament there every year.

Chesneau et Pierre Thévenin
FFF
New Golf de Deauville - H
Saint-Arnoult
Deauville (Calvados)
Tel.: 02 31 14 24 24
Architectes: Tom Simpson et
Henry Cotton
FFF

Nîmes-Campagne - 18 holes
Route de Saint-Gilles
Nîmes (Gard)
Tel.: 04 66 70 17 37
Architectes: Donald
Harradine
FF

Nîmes-Vacquerolles - 18 holes
Route de Sauve
Nîmes (Gard)
Tel.: 04 66 23 33 33
Architect: Bill Baker
FF

Omaha Beach - 27 holes - H
Ferme Saint-Sauveur
Port-en-Bessin (Calvados)
Tel.: 02 31 21 72 94
Architect: Yves Bureau
FF

Orléans-Limère - 18 holes - H
Allée de la Pomme de Pin
Ardon (Loiret)
Tel.: 02 38 63 89 40
Architect: Cabell Robinson
FFF

Paris International Club - 18 holes
18, route du Golf
Baillet-en-France (Val d'Oise)
Tel.: 01 34 69 90 00

Architect: Jack Nicklaus
FFF
Pau - 18 holes
Rue du Golf
Billère (Pyrénées-Atlantiques)
Tel.: 05 59 13 18 56
Architect: Willie Dunn
FF

Pléneuf-Val André - 18 holes
Pléneuf-Val André (Côtes
d'Armor)
Tel.: 02 96 63 01 12
Architect: Alain Prat
FF

Plœmeur-Océan - 18 holes
Saint-Jude Kerman
Plœmeur (Morbihan)
Tel.: 02 97 32 81 82
FF

Pont-Royal - 18 holes - H
Mallemort (Bouches-du-Rhône)
Tel.: 04 90 57 40 79
Architect: Severiano
Ballesteros
FFF

Prée-La Rochelle - 18 holes
Marsilly (Charente-Maritime)
Tel.: 05 46 01 24 42
Architect: Olivier Brizon
FF

Prieuré de Ganay - 27 holes
Saint-Laurent-Nouan (Loir-et-Cher)
Tel.: 02 54 87 26 24
Architect: Jim Shirley
F

Prunevelle - 18 holes
Dampierre-sur-le-Doubs
(Doubs)
Tel.: 03 81 98 11 77
FF

Rebetz - 18 holes
Route de Noailles
Chaumont-en-Vexin (Oise)
Tel.: 03 44 49 15 54
Architect: Jean-Pascal Fourès
FFF

Reims - 18 holes
Château des Dames de
France

Gueux (Marne)
Tel.: 03 26 05 46 10
Architect: Michael Fenn
FF

Rhin-Chalampé - 18 holes
Ile du Rhin
Chalampé (Haut-Rhin)
Tel.: 03 89 26 07 86
Architect: Donald Harradine
FFF

Royal Mougins - 18 holes
424, avenue du Roi
Mougins (Alpes-Maritimes)
Tel.: 04 92 92 49 69
Architect: Robert Von Hagge
FFF

Royan - 18 holes
Maine Gaudin
Saint-Palais-sur-Mer (Charente-Maritime)
Tel.: 05 46 23 16 24
Architect: Robert Berthet
FF

Sablé-Solesmes - 27 holes
Route de Pincé
Sablé-sur-Sarthe (Sarthe)
Tel.: 02 43 95 28 78
Architect: Michel Gayon
FF

Saint-Aubin - 27 holes
Route du Golf
Saint-Aubin (Essonne)
Tel.: 01 69 41 25 19
Architect: Robert Berthet
FF

Saint-Cyprien - 27 holes - H
Mas d'Huston
Saint-Cyprien Plage (Pyrénées
Orientales)
Tel.: 04 68 37 63 63
Architectes: Tom Wright et
Barry Tomlinson
FF

Saint-Donat - 18 holes
270, route de Cannes
Plan-de-Grasse (Alpes-Maritimes)
Tel.: 04 93 09 76 60
Architect: R.Trent Jones Jr
FFF

Saint-Endréol - 18 holes
Route de Bagnols-en-Forêt
La Motte (Var)
Tel.: 04 94 51 89 89
Architect: Michel Gayon
FFF

Saint-Etienne - 18 holes
62, rue Saint-Simon
Saint-Etienne (Loire)
Tel.: 04 77 32 14 63
Architect: Thierry Sprecher
FF

Saint-Germain - 27 holes
Route de Poissy
Saint-Germain-en-Laye
(Yvelines)
Tel.: 01 39 10 30 30
Architect: Harry S. Colt
FFF

Saint-Jean-de-Monts - 18 holes
- H
Avenue des Pays de Loire
Saint-Jean-de-Monts (Vendée)
Tel.: 02 51 58 82 73
Architect: Yves Bureau
FF

Saint-Laurent - 18 holes - H
Plöemel
Auray (Morbihan)
Tel.: 02 97 56 85 18
Architectes: Michael Fenn et
Yves Bureau

Saint-Nom-la-Bretèche - 36
holes
Hameau de la Tuilerie Bignon
Saint-Nom-la-Bretèche
(Yvelines)
Tel.: 01 30 80 04 40
Architect: Fred Hawtree
Sur invitation d'un membre

Sainte-Baume - 18 holes
Domaine de Châteauneuf
Nans-les-Pins (Var)
Tel.: 04 94 78 60 12
Architect: Robert Berthet
FF

Sainte-Maxime - 18 holes - H
Route du Débarquement
Sainte-Maxime (Var)
Tel.: 04 94 55 02 02

Architect: Donald Harradine
FFF

Seignosse - 18 holes - H
Avenue du Belvédère
Seignosse (Landes)
Tel.: 05 58 41 68 30
Architect: Robert Von Hagge
FFF

Servanes - 18 holes
Domaine de Servanes
Mouriès (Bouches-du-Rhône)
Tel.: 04 90 47 59 95
Architectes: Thierry Sprecher
et Gery Watine
FF

Soufflenheim-Baden Baden -
27 holes
Allée du Golf
Soufflenheim (Bas-Rhin)
Tel.: 03 88 05 77 00
Architect: Bernhard Langer
FFF

Sperone - 18 holes
Domaine de Sperone
Bonifacio (Corse)
Tel.: 04 95 73 17 13
Architect: Robert Trent Jones
Sr
FFF

Taulane - 18 holes - H
RN 85
La Martre (Var)
Tel.: 04 93 60 31 30
Architect: Gary Player
FFF

Tignes - 18 holes
Le Val Claret
Tignes (Savoie)
Tel.: 04 79 06 37 42
Architect: Philippe Valant
FF

Toulouse-Palmola - 18 holes
Route d'Albi
Buzet-sur-Tarn (Haute-
Garonne)
Tel.: 05 61 84 20 50
Architect: Michael Fenn
FFF

Toulouse-Seilh - 36 holes - H
Route de Grenade

Seilh (Haute-Garonne)
Tel.: 05 62 13 14 14
Architectes: Jean Garaialde et
Jérémy Pern
FF

Touraine - 18 holes
Château de la Touche
Ballan-Miré (Indre-et-Loire)
Tel.: 02 47 53 20 28
Architect: Michael Fenn
FF

Tours-Ardrée - 18 holes
Saint-Antoine-du-Rocher (Indre-
et-Loire)
Tel.: 02 47 56 77 38
Architect: Olivier Brizon
FF

Valescure - 18 holes
Route du Golf
Saint-Raphaël (Var)
Tel.: 04 94 82 40 46
Architect: Lord Aschcomb
FFF

Vaugouard - 18 holes - H
Fontenay-sur-Loing (Loiret)
Tel.: 02 38 89 79 00
Architectes: Marc Adam et
Patrick Fromanger
FFF

Vichy - 18 holes
Bellerive-sur-Allier (Allier)
Tel.: 04 70 32 39 11
Architect: Arnaud Massy
FF

Villarceaux - 18 holes

*In Servannes at the foot of the
Alpilles, a pretty stroll can be
taken to the song of cicadas.*

Château du couvent
Chaussy (Val d'Oise)
Tel.: 01 34 67 73 83
Architect: John Baker
FFF

Vittel - 36 holes - H
Avenue de l'Ermitage
Vittel (Vosges)
Tel.: 03 29 08 59 40
FF

Volcans - 18 holes
Orcines (Puy-de-Dome)
Tel.: 04 73 62 15 51
Architect: Lucien Roux
FF

Wantzenau - 18 holes
CD 302
Wantzenau (Bas-Rhin)
Tel.: 03 88 96 37 73
Architect: Jean Garaialde et
Jérémy Pern
FFF

Wimereux - 18 holes
Avenue François Mitterrand
Wimereux (Pas-de-Calais)
Tel.: 03 21 32 43 20
Architectes: Campbell et
Hutchinson